Morning Musings

QUIET TIME REFLECTIONS

EMILY TYLER AND AIMÉE WALKER

The Devoted Collective
Auckland, New Zealand
www.thedevotedcollective.org

ISBN Hardcover 978-0-473-65922-6

Cover design by Holly Robertson at Design by Rocket
Edited by Vicki Bentley

Cataloguing in Publishing Data
Title: Morning Musings
Authors: Emily Tyler and Aimée Walker
Subjects: Devotions, Christian life, Spirituality

A copy of this title is held at the National Library of New Zealand

KNOW THIS: GOD, YOUR GOD, IS
GOD INDEED, A GOD YOU CAN
DEPEND UPON.

DEUTERONOMY 7:9 MSG

Hi friend,

We're so glad you've picked up this book.

This book is 'us'. From the mugs we like to start our days with to confessions about the state of our laundry, it's real life. It's the struggles we've faced, the lessons we've lived, and the Scriptures that have shaped us and now fill these pages. We want to see you grow in faith and be drawn closer to the Father's heart as you ground yourself in His truth. We want you to experience *everything* He has for you. So we're giving you our best—sausage fingers and all, this book is our offering to you.

From the outset, we want to give you grace to use this book in a way that suits your season. Whether you snack or feast; read and run, or take your time going down rabbit trails exploring the Scriptures we've shared, we pray you encounter Jesus on every page and hear Holy Spirit's voice loudest as you head into your day.

May these words spur your heart to love the Lord with all that you are, right where you are.

Emily & Aimée
xo

Contents

Lead Me to the Rock

AIMÉE

The cliffs towered over me as I walked along the shoreline, hues of rock and clay melding together to form impressive patterns. Big and sturdy, they had withstood the battering tides and now remained as a symbol of strength and stability.

I'd escaped to the beach hoping to find some respite. I was overwhelmed by the things I was facing and trying to figure out how the various threads of my story fitted together. But it felt like the more I pondered, the heavier my heart became. As I stood beneath these cliffs, I knew that God was challenging me to adjust my focus. David's cry in the Psalms echoed in my spirit: "When my heart is overwhelmed, lead me to the rock that is higher than I" (Psalm 61:2 NKJV).

In the midst of his own battles, David knew who had the power to save him. He would go on to say: "For You have been a shelter for me. A strong tower from the enemy. I will abide in Your tabernacle forever; I will trust in the shelter of Your wings" (vv.3-4 NKJV). God's past faithfulness gave him confidence that the Lord would continue to protect and provide for him. And so, he set his focus on dwelling with God.

That day, there were little to no signs of life at the base of the cliffs. But as I lifted my gaze, I noticed that on their heights, foliage flourished. When we fix our gaze downwards, only focusing on our problems, on our hurts and our worries; it is easy to become overwhelmed—for our hearts to tire and fail. But when we lift our focus and look to the Rock that is higher; when we make Jesus the One that we abide in, not only is life released, it is sustained. New and beautiful things are able to grow.

In life, we don't get to control everything that happens to us, but we do get to choose our focus. Today, intentionally look to the Rock who is higher, to the One who is not moved by the tides of life: Jesus. Choose to abide in His presence, enjoying His shelter and protection so that like the foliage I saw flourishing on the cliff tops, you can be infused with life—*His life*.

THEY REMEMBERED THAT GOD
WAS THEIR ROCK, THAT GOD MOST
HIGH WAS THEIR REDEEMER.

PSALM 78:35

Father, I choose today to turn my focus upward and to keep my attention fixed on You, the Rock who is Higher. You are the place where I dwell— my shelter and my strong tower—and You make beautiful things grow in the soil of my life.

Designed to Thrive

EMILY

I am no expert when it comes to plants, so on visiting a garden centre, I took along my learned friend to advise me on which plants might be suitable for the house. She pointed out some different possibilities, but the description on one plant stopped me in my tracks: "Thriving when neglected, the ZZ plant accepts low-light areas and is also drought-tolerant."

I'm not sure that's my experience. There are times when I have felt neglected or like I've had to survive in the dark and tolerate painful situations, but instead of thriving, I wilted and wondered how much longer I'd be able to cope.

This is not the life God designed for His children. You and I were designed to thrive. We weren't designed for neglect, darkness, and exposure to fierce elements. We were made for the abundant life, to be cherished and cared for in perfect relationship with the ultimate Creator-Gardener. That's why God doesn't overlook us or leave us in the dark. Unlike the ZZ plant, we were designed to live and breathe and function in the full light of His presence. So much so, that God gave us His Shekinah Glory, the manifest presence of His Spirit within us, so we can shine His light into other people's darkness too.

The instructions also indicated the ZZ plant should only be watered once dry. We, however, need daily watering, nourishment, sustenance, and filling. We must come to the One who not only offers, but is Himself the source of the Living Water we seek (John 4:10). When we "come to the waters" (Isaiah 55:1), we receive the very life we need to thrive. For the one who delights in the Lord and "meditates on his law" daily will be "like a tree planted by streams of water, which yields its fruit in season and whose leaf does not wither—whatever they do prospers" (Psalm 1:2-3).

If I were a plant, that's the kind of description I would want on my label. And the good news is, it's possible for us to know this kind of full, free, and prosperous life. We just need to remember we're not ZZ plants. Rather than choosing to remain in low-light, droughty, dry locations, we can instead turn towards the light of Jesus' presence, where we will be tended to, cared for, cherished, and watered with all the fullness of life.

JESUS ANSWERED HER, "IF YOU KNEW THE GIFT OF GOD AND WHO IT IS THAT ASKS YOU FOR A DRINK, YOU WOULD HAVE ASKED HIM AND HE WOULD HAVE GIVEN YOU LIVING WATER."

JOHN 4:10

Father, I believe I was created for the abundant life and that You've provided everything needed for me to thrive. I come to You today for the nourishment and sustenance I need, knowing You will enable me to prosper and be fruitful in every season.

Simply Ask

AIMÉE

They held my hand, gently guiding me upstairs to where my 'surprise' awaited. Candles had been lit, my fine china laid out with a cup of tea and brownie accompanied by sweet notes. They closed the door, telling me to enjoy some time to myself—and that I did!

I felt so blessed by the efforts my children went to that afternoon to do something nice for me, however, there was a 'but' to the experience. You see, their efforts had not been entirely intended to bless me, but rather to 'butter-me-up'. There was something that they wanted me to do for them, and their treats were meant to pave the way for their request and ensure their success.

While I did admire their forethought and planning, the result was that their care for me seemed calculated rather than genuine. It left me feeling somewhat manipulated. I would have preferred for them to have simply asked me for what they wanted. In that moment, I wondered if I was being given a glimpse into how our Heavenly Father can feel when we approach Him like this with our own needs and desires.

We have been given access to the throne room of God and invited to boldly come and receive the mercy and grace we need (Hebrews 4:16 and 10:19). There is no need to play games, twist His arm, or attempt to earn His favour—we simply need to ask. In John 16, Jesus tells us that whatever we ask for in His name, the Father will give us (v.23). He also tells us why we can have such confidence, saying, "In that day you will ask in my name. I am not saying that I will ask the Father on your behalf. No, the Father Himself loves you because you have loved me and have believed that I came from God" (vv.26-27).

Love is the language of prayer—not performance. It is our love for Jesus that gives us access to the Father, and it is the Father's love for us and for His Son which releases answers.

What do you need today? Simply and boldly come before the Father and ask Him for it, trusting that in His great love for you He will answer—and answer well.

LET US THEN APPROACH GOD'S THRONE OF GRACE WITH CONFIDENCE, SO THAT WE MAY RECEIVE MERCY AND FIND GRACE TO HELP US IN OUR TIME OF NEED.

HEBREWS 4:16

Father, I draw near and approach Your throne of grace today with confidence to receive the help that I need. I love You, and I know that You love me. I do not need to earn your favour—I already have it.

Pools of Poison

EMILY

I once got an 'arachnidism' on my finger. In other words, I was bitten by a poisonous spider, but I learnt a new word so, there you go. Initially, I had an extreme wave of nausea. This was followed by feeling like I'd got a graze on my finger. It wasn't until the next morning that I could clearly see two marks where the fangs had pierced my skin and to the side, a small sac of venom. Nice.

The kids were momentarily excited to see if I would develop any super-spidey powers. They soon realised having an arachnidism isn't much fun, because the thing about venom is that it's not good for you. It's poison. And no one wants a pool of poison hanging out underneath their skin. I had a front row seat to why as my wound festered and grew.

The venom ate away at my flesh and caused a hole to appear in my finger. I can now relate to Psalm 38 in a whole new way: "My wounds fester and are loathsome. . . my friends and companions avoid me because of my wounds" (v.5, 11). No more hand holding for me.

Like spiders, snakes are known for their venom. And we all know that Satan was first depicted as a serpent. The devil is slithering around eager to inject his venom into you. He wants to see the effect of sin take root and slowly erode and poison you. He wants to take what was once healthy and contaminate it, so that you experience pain, lose what is good, and are left on a slippery slope towards isolation, pain, and ultimately death.

David's wounds depicted in Psalm 38 are caused by his sin. It is because of his sinful folly that they fester. Our sin *will* destroy us. And yet, "if we confess our sins, he is faithful and just to forgive us our sins and to cleanse us from all unrighteousness" (1 John 1:9 ESV).

Just like my wound required me to be vigilant, keeping it clean and taking my antibiotics to guard against further infection, we also need to be vigilant about the poison of sin in our lives. Do not attempt to leave it untreated. Clean the wound through confession and repentance, and allow the balm of Jesus' forgiveness to cleanse and completely restore you.

CLEANSE ME WITH HYSSOP, AND I
WILL BE CLEAN: WASH ME, AND I
WILL BE WHITER THAN SNOW.

PSALM 51:7

Father, thank You that You are faithful to forgive
me and to cleanse me of all sin and shame. I, too, will
be faithful to come into Your presence and repent
so that the enemy cannot poison my life with sin.

Spend Your Time Well

AIMÉE

One of my girls is a spender. The moment she has managed to accumulate even just a couple of dollars she's begging to go spend them. I find myself having to constantly remind her that if she spends now, then she is delaying being able to get what she really wants. She's learning she must determine what matters and plan accordingly, because money, like any other resource, is finite and requires stewarding. It cannot be endlessly stretched, and neither can our time.

My preference has always been to say "yes" when people ask something of me. However, experience has taught this recovering people-pleaser that I can't say yes to all the requests and opportunities that come my way, no matter how good they are, because every yes spends my time.

It's easy to fall into the trap of believing that 'no' is a negative word—that it is shutting off opportunities, denying ourselves pleasure, closing doors, and causing us to disappoint and offend people. However, I have come to understand that every no is really a 'yes' to something else, and ultimately, it is a yes to what God is asking me to prioritise.

In Luke 4:42-44, Jesus models this for us. He has been busy healing the sick and setting people free in the town of Capernaum. What He was doing was a good thing, a great thing actually, and understandably, the people wanted Him to stay with them. But Jesus was mindful of what God had sent Him to do, which was to proclaim and demonstrate the good news in more than one place. So when they try to keep Him from leaving, He says, "I must proclaim the good news of the kingdom of God to the other towns also, because that is why I was sent."

I have no doubt that His 'no' disappointed the people of Capernaum. But if He had said yes to staying, He would have been saying no to the Father, which in turn would have caused fewer people to hear the good news of God's love. We must learn from Jesus' example and obediently invest our time into the people and priorities that God has for us in this season so that His Kingdom purposes can be realised in and through us. Only then will our time be well spent.

TEACH US TO NUMBER OUR DAYS, THAT WE MAY GAIN A HEART OF WISDOM. . . MAY THE FAVOUR OF THE LORD OUR GOD REST ON US; ESTABLISH THE WORK OF OUR HANDS FOR US – YES, ESTABLISH THE WORK OF OUR HANDS.

PSALM 90:12 & 17

Father, I choose today to spend my time well and to allow You to order and establish the work of my hands. I will seek Your pleasure and Your purposes in all that I do, following obediently where You lead.

Life in the Light

EMILY

When winter approaches, the darker days start to take their toll, and I really notice those moments when the sun seeps through the clouds. Like a cat on a mission, I stalk out any stream of sunlight in the house and position myself right in the centre, ready to reap the benefits.

Our kitchen bench gets all the morning sun. If I dwell there at the table with my back to the window for long enough, I notice that it's not only me who gets warmer, but my surroundings increase in warmth too. I gradually feel myself thaw—physically and emotionally. It turns out that being warm physically also makes me a warmer person to be around.

However, if I'm constantly moving—getting up and down, fetching things, fixing things, busying myself—then the sun can't have the same effect on me. To benefit from its warmth, I need to be still and dwell in its presence rather than move about in the shadows and dark.

Luke writes that it is God's gift of tender mercy which breaks upon us. Just as the sun on a winter's day feels like a gift, so too is His light from heaven a present that warms, thaws, and gives life and light to the darkened areas of our lives and soul. All this He does to "guide us to the path of peace" (Luke 1:78-79 NLT).

The morning sun changes my posture and outlook on the day. In the same way, the presence of God alters us (and in turn, our surroundings) to become warmer, more radiant, peace-filled people. God hasn't left us in a perpetual winter of cold, dark, and grey. We were made for life in the centre of His light and power, warmth and love. The power of His presence changes our countenance, shifts our perspective, and resets our focus.

Dwelling in the presence of the sun and stilling myself long enough to benefit from its warmth always leads to a better day. *How much more is that the case when we choose to seek out and dwell in the centre of the True Light from heaven?* If you're lacking peace at the moment, take some time to sit in the centre of the Son's presence and allow Him to guide you "to the path of peace."

BECAUSE OF GOD'S TENDER MERCY, THE MORNING LIGHT FROM HEAVEN IS ABOUT TO BREAK UPON US, TO GIVE LIGHT TO THOSE WHO SIT IN DARKNESS AND IN THE SHADOW OF DEATH, AND TO GUIDE US TO THE PATH OF PEACE.

LUKE 1:78–79 NLT

Father, I choose today to be still and to position myself in the light of Your presence. I reset my perspective to align my focus with Yours; the paths I walk lead to peace.

Hot Bread

AIMÉE

Life had caught up with me. An intense period of writing and ministry had collided with big changes in our family meaning everyone—and I mean *everyone*—needed me! My sleep deprived body just didn't have the reserves to keep pushing through, and this constant state of exhaustion was having an impact on every aspect of my life—physically and spiritually.

Elijah also understood what it felt like to reach the end of yourself.

Despite being responsible for calling down rain and ending a three year drought for Israel, in 1 Kings 19 we read that a threat has been made against his life because his actions have exposed Baal as the false and powerless god that he was. You might think this mighty man of God, who had just played a key role in performing not one but two miracles, would have responded in faith, but instead he runs away. Deeply depressed, he tells God he's had enough—he simply can't do it anymore. Then he falls asleep under a tree.

It encourages me no end that even the heroes of our faith got tired too, but it's God's response to Elijah that encourages me even more. God does not berate Elijah or give him a pep talk, but sends an angel to minister to him. The angel tends to Elijah's physical needs, providing him with freshly baked bread and water before leaving him to continue sleeping. When the angel returns, he wakes Elijah telling him, "Get up and eat, for the journey is too much for you" (v.7).

Sometimes, the journey is too much for us too. We get tired and worn down by all that life asks of us, but the beautiful truth is that God wants to meet us in that place of weariness and minister to our bodies *and* our spirits. He knows that strength flows in our life with both of these aspects are tended to. So He invites us to rest and receive the gift of Himself—for the bread that He offers us is Christ, the Bread of Life, and the water, His very Spirit.

Where does it all feel too much for you today? Intentionally slow down. Nourish your body with good food, and as you do, consider the meal that God prepared for Elijah and the One that it points to. Feast on His provision, and let Him make you strong for the journey that you find yourself on.

COME TO ME, ALL YOU WHO ARE
WEARY AND BURDENED, AND I WILL
GIVE YOU REST. TAKE MY YOKE
UPON YOU AND LEARN FROM ME,
FOR I AM GENTLE AND HUMBLE IN
HEART, AND YOU WILL FIND REST
FOR YOUR SOULS.

MATTHEW 11:28-29

Father, I bring You my weariness today knowing
that You are gentle and humble and care for
my well-being. I receive Your gift of rest and I
feast on the provision of all that Christ has done
for me, nourishing both my body and my spirit.

Don't Fake It

EMILY

Several years ago in the UK, two friends won four million pounds on a scratch card. They danced around the shop, hugging one another and celebrating. Their joy, which was captured on video camera, was undeniable. Never had you seen such delight! However, when they sought to claim the money, one of the individuals let slip that he didn't have a bank account to deposit the winnings into.

You see, the pair had bought the ticket fraudulently with a stolen credit card. The authorities investigated and eventually the two ended up in jail—*without* their four million. The lesson from their story is this: you don't get the prize if you're pretending to be someone else.

I think sometimes I fall prey to thinking I need to be like someone else to be truly 'Christian'. But the reality is when we come to Christ, we get to be a new person, a new creation. Paul tells us that, "The old life is gone; a new life emerges!" (2 Corinthians 5:17 MSG). We don't become new through our ability to fake it till we make it. We don't get this new life by pretending to be someone we're not. It's not about going through the motions of being a Christian whether that's attending church, saying the 'right' things, or acting like other Christians that we see and respect.

It's a gift.

A total transformation that we are not in control of. It's all about who Jesus is, what He has done, and what He promises to do in us. And yet, not everyone who calls Jesus "Lord" will enter the kingdom of heaven. To some, He will "tell them plainly, 'I never knew you. Away from me, you evildoers'" (Matthew 7:21-23).

There's no point trying to fake it until we make it. Jesus tells us that "only the one who does the will of my Father in heaven" (v.21) will be with Him for eternity. Obedience is a sure way to know you're not faking your faith. It's not your job to do the transforming; Jesus will take care of that. Your job is to simply follow Him.

THEREFORE, IF ANYONE IS IN CHRIST, THE NEW CREATION HAS COME: THE OLD HAS GONE, THE NEW IS HERE!

2 CORINTHIANS 5:17

Father, I believe I am a new creation. I receive this gift of transformation and in all I think, say, and do, I choose to submit my will to follow and obey You. I know You will be faithful to complete what You have begun in me.

Running on Empty

AIMÉE

"E is for enough," my mum always used to tell us when the fuel light came on to warn her that the petrol tank was nearing empty. I've recalled her words more times than I can count over the years. When my own fuel light's been on longer than it should be, and I've wondered how we'll make ends meet, they've helped me to remember that though I see emptiness, God has and is enough for me.

Limitations weigh on us all in some way at some point in time. Whether it's the overdrawn bank balance, the situation at work that is overwhelming us, or the child we just can't seem to connect with, we see the flashing 'E' of emptiness in neon lights and allow our inadequacies to define and constrain us. God has to continually remind me that life in the Kingdom is not based on what we do or don't have, but on what *He* has. We are called to live our lives rooted in the truth of His abundance and goodness.

The apostle Paul reminds us of this truth, declaring, "I know now how to live when things are difficult and I know how to live when things are prosperous. In general and in particular I have learned the secret of facing either poverty or plenty. I am ready for anything through the strength of the One who lives within me" (Philippians 4:11-13 Phillips).

These are often quoted words but *do we know what it is to live them? Do we honestly believe that Christ is enough for every season and every situation?*

I have learned by repeated experience what it is to allow Him to be enough when I lack, but Christ's invitation is to a life of dependence on His power even when it's something I feel like I've got under control. It's for the places that I think, *I've got this*—where resources and talents abound—as much as it's for the places that I wrestle and struggle in. It's always about His strength and empowering grace. So whether your fuel tank is full or running on fumes, may 'E' remind you today that He truly is enough.

AND MY GOD WILL MEET ALL YOUR
NEEDS ACCORDING TO THE RICHES
OF HIS GLORY IN CHRIST JESUS. TO
OUR GOD AND FATHER BE GLORY
FOR EVER AND EVER. AMEN.

PHILIPPIANS 4:19-20

Father, I believe that You have and are enough
for me. I enter today confident that no matter
what it holds, I will be empowered and resourced
by Your Spirit to navigate it well for Your glory.

You're Forgetting Who I Am

EMILY

One of my kids was on the struggle-bus recently. He was having a very hard time realising that the world was not against him and that, despite how he felt, I was actually being super kind, gracious, and loving. In the middle of our conversation, wanting him to grasp and understand just how much I loved him, I said, "Child, I think you're forgetting who I am." Instantly in that moment, I felt the Holy Spirit whisper the exact same thing to me.

"Child... I think you're forgetting who I am."

When things aren't going how we expect them to; when life is difficult, hormones are raging, or we receive terrible news, how often do we rage or sulk at God, metaphorically slam doors, or hold Him at arm's length? How often do we shut Him down and refuse to engage out of a place of pain? How often do we wonder how on earth can God love us when life is unfolding as it is?

Child... I think you're forgetting who He is.

He *is* love.

He is slow to anger and abounding in love. His desire is to lavish His inseparable love on you. He loves you with an everlasting, never-stopping, always-enduring love because you are His treasured possession, His chosen child.

You are precious in His sight and you are loved with an almighty, death-defying love. You are safe and secure in that love. You are rooted and grounded in that love. That love is higher, wider, deeper, and stronger than you can comprehend, and it is expansive enough to cover you and carry you through all that you're enduring and feeling and experiencing right now.

When I am distracted from truth, Deuteronomy 7:9 reminds me Who it is I can trust: "Know this: God, your God, is God indeed, a God you can depend upon" (MSG). God sees you in this moment. You are not alone. He is mighty to save, your greatest encourager, your shepherd, friend, and Father. You can depend on Him. He hasn't forgotten about you. So child, don't forget who He is.

SO KNOW THAT THE LORD YOUR GOD IS GOD. HE IS THE FAITHFUL GOD. HE WILL KEEP HIS AGREEMENT OF LOVE FOR A THOUSAND LIFETIMES. HE DOES THIS FOR PEOPLE WHO LOVE HIM AND OBEY HIS COMMANDS.

DEUTERONOMY 7:9 ICB

Father, I recall the truth of who You are. I believe that You are God; that You are trustworthy and dependable and that You are near to me. I root and ground myself in Your immeasurable love; no matter what is happening I will trust You.

Own Your Zone

AIMÉE

"You need to own your zone," my friend reminded me as we laughed over her daughters discovering the notes she'd placed under their mattresses declaring, "This child belongs to God." It was a timely exhortation, as truth be told, I was feeling more victim than victor at the time. I needed the nudge that God had given me His authority—His very Spirit within me to empower and instruct me.

When Nehemiah returned to Jerusalem to rebuild her walls, he was met with opposition. People came to mock and ridicule his work, accusing him of rebelling against the king. It sounds like an all-too-familiar scenario to me. As we build our lives the enemy taunts us with feelings of inadequacy; he lies to us time and time again, causing us to question whether we really heard God—whether we're doing this thing 'right'.

Nehemiah refused to entertain their words. He stood firm in what God had called him to do, telling them, "The God of heaven will make us prosper, and we his servants will arise and build, but you have no portion or right or claim in Jerusalem" (Nehemiah 2:20). Nehemiah turned his focus first to the truth of who God is, allowing this to embolden him for the task that lay ahead. But he also rebuked his enemies and reminded them that they had no authority in this situation—only the people of God did. It wasn't the only time he would need to do this. Their work was continually met with opposition, but each time, Nehemiah remained resolute, enabling them to not only complete their work, but to do so in a mere fifty-two days!

What are you building (or rebuilding as it may be) in this season? Maybe it is your marriage, your family, your health, your finances, or your faith. Whatever it is, 'own your zone'. Refuse to entertain the lies of the enemy, stand firm in your God-given authority, and do the work He is asking you to do, confident that He will cause you to prosper.

AND I AM CERTAIN THAT GOD, WHO BEGAN THE GOOD WORK WITHIN YOU, WILL CONTINUE HIS WORK UNTIL IT IS FINALLY FINISHED ON THE DAY WHEN CHRIST JESUS RETURNS.

PHILIPPIANS 1:6 NLT

Father, I commit today to 'own my zone'. I will arise and build with authority where You are asking me to, knowing that You will make me prosper. I believe that You will bring the work You are doing in me and through me to completion.

Apprenticed to the Master

EMILY

I'm quite partial to watching a good hospital drama on television. I watched one episode where a patient died on the operating table because the attending doctor didn't wait for the surgeon to arrive. The subordinate believed that since they'd previously watched the master at work, they could now do it themselves—without the presence of the surgeon. They'd got a little too big for their boots.

On the other hand, Moses knew all too well the importance of only moving when the Master was present: "If your Presence does not go with us, do not send us up from here" (Exodus 33:15). He was aware that despite being God's appointed leader of the Israelites, success would only be found with the Lord's guidance and, more importantly, His presence.

Just as an attending is an apprentice to a surgeon, so, too, are we apprentices to the ultimate Master, Jesus. Jesus tells us that we will do greater things than He has done, not because we have read all about it, or even because we have witnessed Him at work personally, but because He has sent One who will help us and be with us forever—One who "lives with you and will be in you" (John 14:17). When we believe in Jesus, we receive His very presence to be with us eternally, we receive the Holy Spirit to be our counsellor and guide.

It's easy to begin making plans and resolutions for all we want to achieve. It's easy to start determining a long list of what we will do, who we will be, where we will go, how we will change. But as I've reflected on a season of things being stripped back, it's made me more determined than ever to be like Moses as I head into each day and to declare: *Lord, if Your presence does not go with me, do not send me on from here.*

Unlike the apprentice who cannot always be with the attending, we can daily keep our eyes on the Master because He will never leave the room. Through His Spirit our ever-present, loving guide will moment by moment lead us on.

MOSES SAID, "IF YOUR PRESENCE DOESN'T TAKE THE LEAD HERE, CALL THIS TRIP OFF RIGHT NOW. HOW ELSE WILL IT BE KNOWN THAT YOU'RE WITH ME IN THIS, WITH ME AND YOUR PEOPLE?

EXODUS 33:15-16A MSG

Father, I will move when You say "move." I am sensitive to Holy Spirit's leading; He is my ever-present advocate and guide. In my planning, decision making, and moving, I submit to His direction so that I might glorify You.

Enjoy God Forever

AIMÉE

The very first question of the Westminster Catechism has long-fascinated me. "What is the chief end of man?" it asks. *The answer?* "Man's chief end is to glorify God, and to enjoy Him forever." The idea that simply enjoying God is a worthy goal in and of itself has always captured my attention. With my wiring, it can be all too easy for me to get so caught up in 'doing' for God—in busily trying to bring Him glory—that I cease to enjoy Him. But I wonder, *Can I truly and fully glorify God if I do not first enjoy Him?*

From the very beginning of time, it has been God's intention that we would delight in being His children. This theme is woven throughout Scripture with its many invitations and commands to delight in and rejoice in God at all times and in all things.

Desiring to enjoy God is not self-seeking, it is worship. And because we have a compulsion to share with others the things that bring us pleasure, it will lead others to worship. As C.S. Lewis once said, "We delight to praise what we enjoy because the praise not merely expresses but completes the enjoyment."

If you are wondering today how you could better glorify God, perhaps the answer lies in slowing down to enjoy Him a little more; in awakening to the many ways He is present in your life. From the first morning rays of light to the way He paints the sky at the close of day, there are so many opportunities for us to behold His wonder and His splendour. As Paul encourages us with this beautiful exhortation: "My beloved ones, don't ever limit your joy or fail to rejoice in the wonderful experience of knowing our Lord Jesus!" (Philippians 3:1 TPT).

There is no limit to the joy that is found in Christ. Today, may we take the time to rejoice in and savour the privilege of knowing Him, and may we share it with those around us that they too may fulfil their true purpose: to glorify God and enjoy Him forever.

REJOICE IN THE LORD ALWAYS. I
WILL SAY IT AGAIN: REJOICE! LET
YOUR GENTLENESS BE EVIDENT TO
ALL. THE LORD IS NEAR.

PHILIPPIANS 4:4-5

Father, I rejoice today in the wonder of knowing
You. I celebrate Your goodness and the many
and varied ways in which You reveal Yourself to
me. I seek to not only glorify You at all times, but
also to enjoy You and to make that joy known.

Don't Miss the View

EMILY

I sat down for lunch and was several mouthfuls in before I realised I was facing the wrong way. You see, we were housesitting for friends in a beautiful home with incredible ocean views. But I had chosen to sit down at the table with my back to the window, facing a blank wall.

In that moment of realisation I had a choice. *Was I going to stand up, rearrange the table, and face the other way? Or would I take the simpler, easier option of not moving?* I chose to move. And it was worth it. The view was amazing—constantly changing and inspiring, there were new things to see and take in at every moment.

The Bible is full of imagery around positioning. Positioning yourself for battle, positioning yourself to wait and see what God will say or do, positioning yourself in relation to others and elevating them ahead of yourself—it matters where we place ourselves.

Positioning is important.

So as you get ready for a new day, what is your position? Have you resorted to the simple and easy option of staying where you are, facing the wrong way, and missing out on the ever-changing view that God has for you? Are you staring at a blank wall and suffering the lack of inspiration, drive, or faith as a result? Or are you prepared to move yourself—to position yourself in the Word, at the feet of Jesus, and in line with Holy Spirit—so that you don't miss out on all that God wants to reveal to you?

We can learn much from Habakkuk regarding posture when it comes to seeing, hearing, and receiving all God wants to reveal to us. He says, "I will take my post; I will position myself on the fortress. I will keep watch to see what the Lord says to me and how he will respond to my complaint" (Habakkuk 2:1 CEB). Like Habakkuk, we might have many complaints from what has gone before, but let's not get stuck in them. Let's take them to God and see what He has to say. Let's be people who are watching and listening for His response. Let's be people who get up and get moving, and who, with the right perspective, position our hearts and ourselves ready to receive all that God has to offer.

DON'T SHUFFLE ALONG, EYES TO THE GROUND, ABSORBED WITH THE THINGS RIGHT IN FRONT OF YOU. LOOK UP, AND BE ALERT TO WHAT IS GOING ON AROUND CHRIST— THAT'S WHERE THE ACTION IS. SEE THINGS FROM HIS PERSPECTIVE.

COLOSSIANS 3:2 MSG

Father, I am prepared to reposition myself to see what You are doing. I will look up; I will watch and listen attentively so that I can understand things from Your perspective and move in unity with You.

Put the Washing On

AIMÉE

I forget about the laundry. Like to the point I have earned a reputation for ruining my children's clothes because they get mouldy in the wash basket.

Believe me, I am not popular when this happens. It's not that I mean to forget about it—it's just that other things feel shinier and more important, and it's tempting to overlook, rush through, or even resent my day in, day out tasks. This hasn't only been true of my 'to-do' list, but also the hard or just plain monotonous seasons I've walked through. But thinking like this only robs me of being present to what God is doing now and causes me to miss the joy of partnering with God where He has me.

Yes, sometimes my heart needs to be reminded now matters—not only because how we steward it shapes tomorrow, but also because it is filled with divine purpose. Now is a powerful opportunity to experience God and serve Jesus right where we are, right as we are.

In Colossians 3:22-24, Paul gave an instruction to slaves that continually challenges me to steward now well. He wrote: "Slaves, obey your earthly masters in everything; and do it, not only when their eye is on you and to curry their favor, but with sincerity of heart and reverence for the Lord. Whatever you do, work at it with all your heart, as working for the Lord, not for human masters, since you know that you will receive an inheritance from the Lord as a reward. It is the Lord Christ you are serving."

Paul's words remind me I do not have to be in my ideal circumstances to serve the Lord, that Christ is my 'master'—the One with power and authority—not my circumstances, and when I do my work unto Christ, every task and season can be a valuable and fruitful one.

Turning my focus towards Christ transforms even the most menial role into a privilege. So today you'll find me in the laundry, faithfully folding and rescuing the clothes from ruin, and remembering that whatever I'm doing, when I'm doing it wholeheartedly for Him, it all matters.

IF ANY OF YOU WANTS TO SERVE
ME, THEN FOLLOW ME. THEN YOU'LL
BE WHERE I AM, READY TO SERVE AT
A MOMENT'S NOTICE. THE FATHER
WILL HONOUR AND REWARD
ANYONE WHO SERVES ME.

JOHN 12:26 MSG

Father, I choose to be present to the tasks
and people before me, recognising that
each of them is an opportunity to serve You
and bring You glory. I believe now matters
and that today is a day of divine purpose.

Keep Eating Those Bananas

EMILY

Bananas are good for you. Rich in potassium which has all sorts of health benefits, eating them can help lower blood pressure and reduce other health risks. They are the fruit of choice for many an athlete and easy to grab on the go. But although I *knew* as a seventeen-year-old that bananas were good for me, the issue was, I just didn't like them.

I didn't like bananas but I *wanted* to like bananas. So, for two weeks every day at school I would try and eat a banana. A tiny little banana. It would take me the entire break. Twenty minutes of nibbling at this awful-tasting, strange consistency of yuck that I knew was good for me.

Fast forward seventeen years, and I *chose* to eat a banana. *Was I trying to inflict some sort of punishment on myself?* No. I actually like bananas now. *The lesson?* Perseverance pays off. Paul wrote that we're not to "become weary in doing good, for at the proper time we will reap a harvest if we do not give up" (Galatians 6:9).

For seventeen years I didn't give up on the idea that one day I might be able to eat a banana and not retch. It might not be bananas for you. You might not like forgiving someone or being a peacemaker when someone has wronged you, but persevere. Maybe it's tithing or being generous with your finances—don't give up. There are many things we don't like doing even though we know they're good for us. Yet we are encouraged to persevere, to keep eating those bananas, because God promises that "at the proper time" we will reap a harvest if we do not give up.

Next time you eat a banana, why not ask Jesus if there's an area of your life that He wants you to persevere in? Your harvest might be just around the corner, it might be seventeen years away, or it might even be stored up for you in heaven—but the promise is there nonetheless. So don't become weary in doing good!

SO LET'S NOT GET TIRED OF DOING
WHAT IS GOOD. AT JUST THE RIGHT
TIME WE WILL REAP A HARVEST OF
BLESSING IF WE DON'T GIVE UP.

GALATIANS 6:9 NLT

Father, I choose to persevere with joy and
faithfulness in the tasks that lie before me today.
I will not give up, but keep doing good and trust
You to reveal the harvest in Your perfect timing.

Do Not Worry

AIMÉE

"Just Enough Light for the Step I'm On." Despite never actually reading the book, this title has remained stuck in my mind. I often think of it when I find myself frustrated trying to figure out what comes next; it reminds me that I don't have to be able to see everything that lies ahead to keep moving forward. I just need enough light to illuminate "the step I'm on."

This truth is not always easy for me to accept. I'd much prefer to have things all planned out and know what lies around the corner, but instead, God invites me to live where the light is and be present to *now*. Jesus put it another way when He said: "Therefore do not worry about tomorrow, for tomorrow will worry about itself. Each day has enough trouble of its own" (Matthew 6:34).

Three times in Matthew 6:25-34, Jesus commands us, "do not worry"—to not be anxious or troubled with cares. Each of these commands is followed with a truth that can set us free from the burden of worrying about what tomorrow may hold.

Do not worry: *You are valuable to the Father* (v.26).
Do not worry: *Your Father knows what you need* (v.32).
Do not worry: *Live in the present where I am, and tomorrow will take care of itself* (v.34).

Jesus speaks to our identity, reminding us we are valuable; He speaks to our needs, reminding us they are seen; and He speaks to our future, reminding us that "God will help [us] deal with whatever hard things come up when the time comes" (v.34 MSG). We are empowered to set aside worry and live in the light of where He is as we "steep [our] lives in God-reality, God-initiative, God-provisions. . . giving our entire attention to what God is doing right now" (vv.33-34 MSG).

God will provide and give us the grace we need along the way, lighting up each step of the path as we reach it. Sometimes, we may only see the one we're on; other times, He may graciously allow us to see several steps ahead, or illuminate a distant horizon to help us navigate the present. Yet if we keep our eyes firmly fixed on Him, there will always be enough light for the step we're on.

"GIVE YOUR ENTIRE ATTENTION TO WHAT GOD IS DOING RIGHT NOW, AND DON'T GET WORKED UP ABOUT WHAT MAY OR MAY NOT HAPPEN TOMORROW. GOD WILL HELP YOU DEAL WITH WHATEVER HARD THINGS COME UP WHEN THE TIME COMES."

MATTHEW 6:34 MSG

Father, I set aside my worries about tomorrow and choose to be present today—to give my full attention to what You are doing right now. I trust You to light up my path and to provide what is needed along the way.

He's Still There

EMILY

According to psychologists, for the first sixteen weeks of their lives, healthy babies don't have the capacity to believe in the object permanence of a thing if they can no longer see it. If you hide a toy they immediately appear to forget it, because they don't believe it exists anymore. Yet, as their brain develops, they reach a stage where they know that just because they can't see the toy anymore doesn't mean it's no longer there, and they'll keep looking for it.

I wonder how often we're like babies when it comes to our dealings with God?

All the time that we see Him at work, all the time we sense His blessing and favour, all the time we see answered prayer, we believe that He's present, real, good, and for us. But the moment He 'disappears from view', we cease to believe His presence is a sure and true thing. We stop trusting in His goodness and faithfulness.

Paul writes to the Corinthians, "I want to remind you of the gospel I preached to you, which you received and on which you have taken your stand. By this gospel you are saved, if you hold firmly to the word I preached to you. Otherwise, you have believed in vain" (1 Corinthians 15:1-2).

Let me remind you too: We are to hold firm to the truth of the gospel, to the words that God has spoken, to the Word, Jesus. When circumstances and the world feed us lies that God doesn't care, that He's not with us, that there's no way out or rescue, we must return to the gospel and the truth of its message. That truth is Jesus.

The original Greek for "hold firm" in this passage is *katechō* which literally means 'to hold down, to retain, to keep in memory'. Let's not be newborn babies anymore when it comes to our faith. Regardless of what you see, let's stand on the truth of the gospel and 'keep in memory' the promises God has given us.

AS FOR THAT IN THE GOOD SOIL,
THEY ARE THOSE WHO, HEARING
THE WORD, HOLD IT FAST IN AN
HONEST AND GOOD HEART, AND
BEAR FRUIT WITH PATIENCE.

LUKE 8:15 ESV

Father, I stand on the truth of the Gospel.
Regardless of what I can or cannot see, I hold
fast to Truth; I hold fast to Jesus. And
as I take hold of Him, Your promises
will be fulfilled and bear fruit in my life.

Set Your Heart on Pilgrimage

AIMÉE

There have been some very big disappointments in my life, and at times all the sacrifices we've made as a family have seemed futile. Discouragement has stymied my faith and caused me to doubt the goodness of God.

Paul exhorts us in Philippians 3 to *press on to take hold of that for which Christ Jesus took hold of us* (v.12), inviting us to "run into His abundance" (v.12 TPT). *But how do we believe there is still abundance for us to experience, let alone take hold of it when disappointment is tempting us to dig our heels in and set up camp?* We must set our hearts on pilgrimage.

In Psalm 84, the psalmist writes: "Blessed are those whose strength is in you, whose hearts are set on pilgrimage. As they pass through the Valley of Baca [weeping], they make it a place of springs. . ." (vv.5-6).

Valleys of weeping are unavoidable in this life, but we were never intended to *stay* in them. We're meant to move through them, and as we do, to experience transformation and redemption. But sometimes we have to ask ourselves if we *want* to move on from the valley. We have to get honest about whether we are willing to set our hearts on pilgrimage.

The Hebrew for 'pilgrimage' refers to someone who has 'the highways of Zion' within their heart. In life, we must determine our desired destination. The psalmist's heart was set on being wherever God was. He yearned for His presence (v.2) and so, no matter what, He kept moving towards his Lord.

I've discovered that when I say yes to being a pilgrim, making Jesus my goal and refusing to be dissuaded from believing that God is good and will be good to *me*, that in time, my valleys of weeping become sweet refreshing springs in my life.

Overcoming disappointment is not something we must conjure up the strength for ourselves. It simply requires us to turn our hearts towards Him and let Him lend us His strength to keep walking through. And step by step, by His grace, we will become stronger and our lives more beautiful. We will go from strength to strength—just like He promises.

HOW LOVELY IS YOUR DWELLING PLACE, LORD ALMIGHTY! MY SOUL YEARNS, EVEN FAINTS, FOR THE COURTS OF THE LORD; MY HEART AND MY FLESH CRY OUTFOR THE LIVING GOD.

PSALM 84:1-2

Father, I set my heart on pilgrimage. I will not let disappointment keep me stuck but will press on to take hold of all that Jesus has for me. Discouragement is not my mantle. Jesus is my goal, my Hope, and the One that my heart yearns for.

Take a Breath

EMILY

Recently one of my children was diagnosed with asthma. During an attack, as the airways constrict and narrow, it becomes difficult to breathe—something I think we can all agree is pretty important! Every system in our body relies on oxygen. Getting sufficient air, sufficient breath, is an essential element of survival. Breathing easily greatly affects our ability to live full and fulfilled lives.

The psalmist exhorts "everything that has breath [to] praise the Lord" (Psalm 150:6), and yet sometimes there are situations in life that constrict and choke our efforts to praise. Challenges and circumstances can leave us breathless, squashed, and struggling.

There are times when asthmatics need assistance to breathe easily. An inhaler can relax the muscles that have tightened around the airways, creating more space and allowing air to flow freely. And there are times when we, too, need assistance to be able to praise. We need to be rescued from the restrictive context we find ourselves in.

But there's good news. No matter what has stolen your breath, God can bring you into a spacious place, and He will rescue you because He delights in you (Psalm 18:19). We might despair when we face our challenge, thinking it's a dead end and that praising from that place is nigh on impossible. But consider God's words to Ezekiel, "I will put breath in you, and you will come to life. Then you will know that I am the Lord" (Ezekiel 37:6).

It is the Spirit of God who made you, it is His breath that gives you life (Job 33:4). He doesn't ask us to strive and produce our own air to breathe—there's enough oxygen for all! He's not asking us to do something that will harm us. He wants you to breathe, to allow your body and mind to slow down enough to remember that He is God. *He* is in control. And He has given us all we need to experience the full, expansive, and free life that Jesus offers.

Don't look at the situation, instead begin praising the One who "gives everyone life and breath and everything else" (Acts 17:25). He's got everything you need to keep going.

Now breathe in and out. Repeat. You're okay. He's got this.

GOD, THE MASTER, TOLD THE DRY
BONES, "WATCH THIS: I'M BRINGING
THE BREATH OF LIFE TO YOU AND
YOU'LL COME TO LIFE. . . YOU'LL
COME ALIVE AND YOU'LL REALISE
THAT I AM GOD!

EZEKIEL 37:5-6 MSG

Father, in You I am fully alive. I have space
to breathe despite my circumstances
because I serve the One who controls
all things and who loves me beyond my
understanding or comprehension. No matter
the situation, I will choose to bring You praise.

Influenced

AIMÉE

During the lockdowns of 2020, I bought a pair of jeans online—isolation causes one to make impulsive and unwise decisions.

I must confess to having been 'influenced' by Instagram. After seeing countless stories on this particular brand, I headed to their site, perused the various styles and descriptors, and selected a pair in my normal size. When they arrived, the cut and colour looked as I had hoped they would—but the jeans themselves looked suspiciously small. Not to be deterred (they were, after all, my 'normal' size), I squeezed myself into them and walked out to show my daughters. Shrieks of laughter ensued when they saw how the jeans accentuated my 'muffin top'.

At this point, I should have packaged them back up to exchange for a larger size. But I didn't. Happy with how they fit in the legs and not able to be bothered with the hassle of booking a return courier mid-pandemic, I decided to see if they would stretch with wear.

This course of action meant much discomfort and the frequent undoing of buttons to provide relief. At the end of a long and uncomfortable day, I was struck by the realisation that my jeans were meant to be conforming to *my* shape and not the other way around. I couldn't help but ponder how often I am prone to do this—to conform myself to my circumstances and perceived expectations, allowing external pressures to shape me.

The truth is, I'm not meant to be conformed to this world (Romans 12:2), but I am called and predestined to be conformed to the image of Christ (Romans 8:29). To conform is 'to act in accordance with, becoming similar in nature, form, or character'. When I resist the pressure to be shaped by the world, instead fixing my attention on God, the Word assures me I will be "changed from the inside out" (Romans 12:2 MSG), able to perceive and respond to God's will for me. And when I walk in accordance with His will, God is able to use this world to shape me for the better—to bring out the best in me.

Who or what are you allowing to shape you?

FIX YOUR ATTENTION ON GOD. YOU'LL BE CHANGED FROM THE INSIDE OUT... UNLIKE THE CULTURE AROUND YOU, ALWAYS DRAGGING YOU DOWN TO ITS LEVEL OF IMMATURITY, GOD BRINGS THE BEST OUT OF YOU, DEVELOPS WELL-FORMED MATURITY IN YOU.

ROMANS 12:2 MSG

Father, I fix my attention on all that You are and all that You have done for me. I have been changed from the inside out, conformed to the image of Christ, and He always brings out the best in me.

Stop Lying Down in the Rain

EMILY

As a child, I remember going on a trip with my parents to London. We rode the bus—it was amazing. When we hopped off, it was raining. I wanted to go one way; they said we needed to go the other. Well, my stubborn, determined toddler brain decided that clearly they didn't understand my way was the best way, so I proceeded to lie down on the wet pavement. Cue the tantrum...

I was *not* going to yield.

Pets on leads sometimes have a similar reaction. They dig in their puppy paws and refuse to yield to the direction you'd have them go. (Especially when it comes to being near a vet.) They don't understand that going in that particular direction is ultimately for their good and not to harm them.

Unfortunately, it doesn't seem like I've grown out of the desire to determine my steps and go my own way. Romans 6:13-14 says:

"Do not let any part of your body become an instrument of evil to serve sin. Instead, give yourselves completely to God, for you were dead, but now you have new life. So use your whole body as an instrument to do what is right for the glory of God. Sin is no longer your master, for you no longer live under the requirements of the law. Instead, you live under the freedom of God's grace" (NLT).

When you give yourself completely to something, you yield to it. You fully embrace it. You surrender to that thing or person. Sin is no longer our master, yet all too often we're laying down in the rain, clinging onto an idea, a practice, a relationship, or a habit that is ultimately going to leave us out in the wet and cold when we have the offer of living fully free for God's glory.

We live under the freedom of God's grace, and that means we have a choice. If you get to a 'give way' or 'yield' sign on the road and choose not to stop then you're a mighty crash waiting to happen. We yield for our own good.

Relinquish your grip on the sin that so easily entangles you and instead, "throw yourselves wholeheartedly and full-time... into God's way of doing things" (Romans 6:13 MSG). Stop lying down in the rain.

OFFER YOURSELVES TO GOD AS
THOSE WHO HAVE BEEN BROUGHT
FROM DEATH TO LIFE; AND OFFER
EVERY PART OF YOURSELF TO
HIM AS AN INSTRUMENT OF
RIGHTEOUSNESS.

ROMANS 6:13B

Father, I relinquish my grip of control and yield to Christ. In all my thoughts, words, and actions, I wholeheartedly surrender to Your way and choose to walk with You. I am fully Yours, and because that is so, I am fully free.

How Far Would You Go?

AIMÉE

His little voice piped up from behind me as we drove to church. "Why do we have cars?" he asked. "So we don't have to walk and we can go lots of places," was my reply. Even as I said it, I wondered just how far I would be willing to travel without my car—I had a feeling that without it, my world would become rather small.

In Mark's gospel, we're told that:

> "Jesus withdrew with his disciples to the lake, and a large crowd from Galilee followed. When they heard about all he was doing, many people came to him from Judea, Jerusalem, Idumea, and the regions across the Jordan and around Tyre and Sidon. Because of the crowd he told his disciples to have a small boat ready for him, to keep the people from crowding him. For he had healed many, so that those with diseases were pushing forward to touch him" (Mark 3:7-10).

Can you imagine this scene? Jesus had simply wanted some downtime, but instead, He's met by crowds so desperate to touch Him that He has to teach them from a boat. This crowd were not only desperate to touch Him, they were also willing to travel a great distance to be with Him. For example, it was 112 kilometres from Judea to Galilee, approximately a two to three day journey on foot; 108 kilometres from Jerusalem; and 193 kilometres from Idumea. The shortest journey was from Tyre, and even that would have taken at least a day. Not to mention they would have had to traverse through difficult and mountainous terrain, and some of the sick would have needed to have been helped if not carried.

As I ponder these distances, I have to ask myself: *How far would I travel to encounter Jesus?* The answer makes me realise just how often I trade encounter for comfort.

We may not have to walk on foot or carry the sick or press through the crowds, but every day we face obstacles and distractions that seek to deter us from meeting with Jesus—from hearing His words and encountering His life. But oh how He longs for us to press through and reach Him so that we, too, can be healed and made whole.

BLESSED ARE THOSE WHO HUNGER
AND THIRST FOR RIGHTEOUSNESS,
FOR THEY WILL BE FILLED.

MATTHEW 5:6

Father, I am desperate for more of You. I hunger and thirst for righteousness—You alone can satisfy and fill me. I will not let comfort dull my desire for Your presence; I press on and in to draw near.

Apple-Eye

EMILY

Bounding into our bedroom early in the morning, our little girl announced, "Daddy, Apple-Eye is here!" It's a term of endearment she often refers to herself as. She knows she is the apple of her father's eye, and with this knowledge comes significance, security, and a strong sense of her self-worth. As her father's "apple-eye," our daughter can count on the fact he is always pleased to see her, he delights to know what's on her heart, and he is quick to envelop her close if she is hurt or sad.

The phrase, "the apple of my eye" predates Shakespeare to as early as AD885. It's used to refer to someone or something that is cherished above all else, and appears a handful of times in Scripture: "In a desert land he found him, in a barren and howling waste. He shielded him and cared for him; he guarded him as the apple of his eye..." (Deuteronomy 32:10).

In Hebrew, the word *ishon* here—'the pupil of the eye'—is the diminutive of the word *iysh*: 'the little man of the eye'. When you look into someone's eye you see your reflection shining back—in essence you are the little man in their eye. Your eye is also one of the most vulnerable parts of your body, requiring protection by blinking or turning away from a ball or a blow. So, to see yourself as the apple of one's eye not only requires physical proximity with that person—a need to be up close and personal with them—but also offers the security of being the object of their protection when you're feeling vulnerable.

My little girl has confidence to step out and try new things when her daddy is near. She knows that her daddy has got her back and will shield, guard, and care for her no matter what. *Why?* As his apple-eye, she knows she is precious to him. In her vulnerability, she can trust that her daddy will look after her, and that in her eyes, he is 'mighty to save'.

Did you know that you are the apple of your Heavenly Father's eye? You are treasured, valued, and prized beyond your comprehension. Come to the Father today knowing that Jesus, the crowning apple of His Father's eye, took on the greatest vulnerability and received the ultimate estrangement because you were worth it to Him.

You, my friend, are God's apple-eye.

IN A DESERT LAND HE FOUND HIM,
IN A BARREN AND HOWLING WASTE.
HE SHIELDED HIM AND CARED FOR
HIM; HE GUARDED HIM AS THE
APPLE OF HIS EYE.

DEUTERONOMY 32:10

Father, I walk in confidence today knowing I am the apple of Your eye and You delight in me. I am precious to You and I trust You to look after me, to protect me, and to show Yourself mighty on my behalf.

Wield Your Authority

AIMÉE

A new family had moved into our street so I'd popped over with some of my famous caramel slices to welcome them. A few weeks later, I found myself knocking on their door again—only this time, my visit wasn't so 'sweet'. It had become apparent that their grandson had a habit of playing explicit, misogynistic music at full volume when they were at work, and I was mad. So mad, that much to my children's embarrassment, I marched over there and told him in no uncertain terms to turn it down, or better yet, turn it off.

The music got turned off and for a few weeks, it looked like our quiet street had returned to normal. Then it started again. Not wanting to be *that* neighbour, forever banging on the door to complain, I began to feel somewhat powerless and resigned to our situation.

But then I heard the whisper of the Spirit, "You have the authority in this situation." So, the next time the music started up, I began to pray, declaring that the enemy had no claim to our street and releasing the attributes of the Kingdom over our home and neighbourhood. Within minutes, the music was turned off.

This became our pattern: He turned his music on, I prayed, the music stopped.

Jesus sits in the place of highest authority, at the right hand of the Father, and *all things* have been placed under His feet. There is nothing that He does not have authority over (Ephesians 1:20-22). And by virtue of our faith in Jesus, we too are now seated in that place of authority (Ephesians 2:6).

We should get angry about the things that are defiling our homes and communities, but we must also remember that the battle does not lie with people. No, as Paul said, "Your hand-to-hand combat is not with human beings, but with the highest principalities and authorities operating in rebellion under the heavenly realms…" (Ephesians 6:12 TPT). The true battle lies in the heavenly realms and it requires a spiritual approach. It requires us to wield the authority Christ has given us with confidence that the weapons He has given us are powerful to tear down strongholds (2 Corinthians 10:4).

You are not powerless. *Where do you need to take back the authority in your life today?*

FOR THE WEAPONS OF OUR WARFARE ARE NOT OF THE FLESH BUT HAVE DIVINE POWER TO DESTROY STRONGHOLDS. WE DESTROY ARGUMENTS AND EVERY LOFTY OPINION RAISED AGAINST THE KNOWLEDGE OF GOD, AND TAKE EVERY THOUGHT CAPTIVE TO OBEY CHRIST.

2 CORINTHIANS 10:4-5 ESV

Father, I believe I am seated in the place of authority with Christ where all things have been placed under His feet. I am not powerless. You have given me divine power to tear down strongholds and to build the Kingdom wherever I go.

Rising Temperatures

EMILY

Did you know that coral is so sensitive that if the temperature changes as little as one or two degrees it will die?

The microscopic algae live within the coral in a mutually beneficial relationship. They keep each other alive. But when the ocean environment changes, the coral has a hissy-fit and expels the algae. This leads to 'coral bleaching' since it's the algae that gives the coral its bright and colourful appearance. More than that, though, if the temperature remains too hot or too cold, the coral won't let the algae back in and it will die.

I think sometimes I run the risk of being too sensitive and expelling those around me who are meant for our mutual edification and growth. Sometimes temperatures in relationships rise and result in barriers being erected and distance created. But, just like the coral, we were made for relationships, and ejecting others never leads to life.

The way to avoid being over-sensitive is to be grounded in an established environment. To be embedded in a strong foundation which ensures that, no matter the rising temperatures, we remain steadfast, secure, and impervious.

It can often feel like we're the ones who have to do the grounding and establishing, that we need to rely on our own strength to avoid heightened sensitivity. But Paul prays instead that we would be established in Christ's love (Ephesians 3:16-18). In his letter to the Romans he says this:

> "After God made that decision of what his children should be like, he
> followed it up by calling people by name. After he called them by name,
> he set them on a solid basis with himself. And then, after getting them
> established, he stayed with them to the end, gloriously completing what he
> had begun" (Romans 8:29-30 MSG).

God will establish us in Himself. He will stay with us. He will complete what He has begun. He will do it. We don't need to over-react when the temperature around us begins to rise, for unlike the coral, our environment doesn't dictate our future. God does. Let's be established—in love.

AND THOSE HE PREDESTINED, HE ALSO CALLED; THOSE HE CALLED, HE ALSO JUSTIFIED; THOSE HE JUSTIFIED, HE ALSO GLORIFIED.

ROMANS 8:30

Father, I root and ground myself in Christ's love for me. I do not rely on my own strength or understanding but trust You to establish me and to complete what You have begun in me.

Infinitely Gentle

AIMÉE

Two pot-plants sit on my kitchen counter. I can't tell you how many times I've nearly killed them, nor how many times my husband has then had to nurse them back to life.

When I look at these plants, I don't see the actual plants as much as I see his diligent care for them. He has never once looked at them and thought they were beyond repair or weren't worth his time and effort. He's simply kept giving them what they need to be able to regain strength and keep growing. The way he has cultivated these plants has been a reminder of how God cares for me.

In Isaiah 42:3, we are told this about Jesus: "A bruised reed He will not break, and a smouldering wick He will not snuff out."

There have been many times in my own journey where I have felt battered and bruised and wondered if I will ever stand tall again. In these seasons, I have discovered that while God is infinitely strong, He is also infinitely gentle. He never uses His power against me but rather harnesses it to build me back up. He is the One who created the heavens and stretched them out, who spread out the earth and gave life to all who walk on it, and yet He stoops down to take me by the hand (vv.5-6).

When Israel felt like this bruised reed and smouldering wick, Isaiah encouraged her with this promise from God: "I, the LORD, have called you for a righteous purpose, and I will take hold of your hand. I will keep you and appoint you to be a covenant for the people and a light for the Gentiles" (v.6). The very ones whose own light had been wavering and becoming faint were destined to be a beacon to the world, to open blind eyes and to set free those held captive in the darkness (v.7).

We have the same hope. Even in our times of frailty and vulnerability, God is still outworking His righteous plans and purposes for our lives. He never gives up on us, but draws us close and pours His strength into us. We can be confident that no matter what, He will not release His hold on us, but will faithfully build us up so that we can then do the same for others.

A BRUISED REED HE WILL NOT
BREAK, AND A SMOULDERING
WICK HE WILL NOT SNUFF OUT.
IN FAITHFULNESS HE WILL BRING
FORTH JUSTICE; HE WILL NOT
FALTER OR BE DISCOURAGED
TILL HE ESTABLISHES JUSTICE ON
EARTH.

ISAIAH 42:3-4A

Father, I thank You for Your gentleness and Your
faithfulness. I know that You have called me for
a righteous purpose, and I stand in wonder that
the same hand that created the heavens holds me
today and will enable me to live out that destiny.

Throw Out the Junk

EMILY

Each time we have to move house, the process reminds me of the junk we accumulate through life. Relocating is an opportunity to take stock, assess what's taking space in your home, and then decide whether it still has value or purpose. *Does it need to stay, is it no longer useful for you but could be a blessing to someone else and can be passed on, or is it actually rubbish and needs to be thrown out?*

It's a time-consuming process to sift, sort, and then execute the decision made for each item and belonging, and it can be a messy process too (things might look worse before they get better). But if you want to move forward, it's necessary.

There's something about getting rid of junk that allows you to clean properly—much like when people say they 'clean' for their cleaners. What they really mean is they need to sort the clutter, make space, and tidy things up so that the deep work of cleaning can actually take place.

When he was getting ready to move, "Jacob told his family and all those who lived with him 'Throw out all the alien gods which you have'" (Genesis 35:2 MSG). I wonder what "alien gods" you've accumulated in your life recently. What things have wormed their way into your home and life and begun to take up space, preventing you from living junk-free and clean? What distractions have stolen your time? What responsibilities have filled your schedules? What unforgiveness, pride, jealousy, or anger is clogging up your heart preventing God from getting in there and doing the deep clean it needs?

Don't be afraid of the mess that might occur in the process of getting rid of your junk. God answered Jacob when he was in trouble, and He'll answer you too. Let Him help you with the sifting, sorting, and cleaning; He *wants* you to reach the promised land free from mess and pain. Let Him take the lead in bringing you Home whole.

"GET RID OF ALL YOUR PAGAN IDOLS, PURIFY YOURSELVES, AND PUT ON CLEAN CLOTHING. . . I WILL BUILD AN ALTAR TO THE GOD WHO ANSWERED MY PRAYERS WHEN I WAS IN DISTRESS. HE HAS BEEN WITH ME WHEREVER I HAVE GONE."

GENESIS 35:2B-3 NLT

Father, I accept Your help to clear the clutter from my life, knowing that as I do, I will encounter You more fully. I strip off that which hinders and the sin that so easily entangles that I may run fast and free in pursuit of Your call.

This is the Day

AIMÉE

It was one of those moments that you want to freeze and somehow etch into your memory so that you don't ever forget it. My two youngest children were sitting next to each other, eating their breakfast in matching thermals, when my son, who was two at the time, then wrapped his chubby arms around his sister and nuzzled his face into hers declaring, "Best friends ever!"

Part of me wanted to jump up, grab the camera, and capture the moment for posterity, but I knew that in doing so, its raw beauty would become contrived. So I simply sat there, drinking in how cute they looked and savouring how they were enjoying one another's company.

I won't lie to you. Sometimes—actually a lot of the time–I struggle to be fully present in my day. My to-do list occupies my mind and my thoughts continually race towards the next thing. Tomorrow can loom larger than today. I get drawn into the lives of people I've never even met as I flick through my social media feeds, all the while failing to engage with the people right in front of me.

In Psalm 118:24, the psalmist writes: "This is the day the Lord has made; let us rejoice and be glad in it" (ESV). If you read through the psalm in its entirety, it is full of moments of both triumph and despair, reminding us that we do not have to wait for life to be perfect to rejoice. We can be glad in 'this day', because we can be glad in Him.

Today, right now, is the day that God has made for us. And from the moment that the sun rises there are countless opportunities for us to bear witness to His grace. Yes, there will be worries and struggles and responsibilities, but there will also be beauty and goodness to marvel at, breathe in, and enjoy.

Today, look for those moments. Rejoice, delight, and exult in what He is doing in your life and where He has you right now. Allow the blessings of this season and His faithfulness to you to be etched into your heart and mind so that you don't ever forget that He is with you or that today is precious.

YOU ARE MY GOD, AND I WILL PRAISE YOU; YOU ARE MY GOD, AND I WILL EXALT YOU. GIVE THANKS TO THE LORD, FOR HE IS GOOD; HIS LOVE ENDURES FOREVER.

PSALM 118:28-29

Father, I believe that You have made today, and regardless of what it holds, I will rejoice in You because You are good. I choose to be present to what You are doing in my life and to exalt You above all.

The Real Deal

EMILY

There's a bird that lives in the bush next to our house, and it has quite the skill for mimicking noises it hears: other birds and animals, alarm clocks, noises from the nearby skate park, mobile phones, or even screaming children. . .

According to my friend Google, mimicry is, 'the action or skill of imitating someone or something, especially in order to entertain or ridicule'. It's fake. It's a trap. Mimicry makes you think it's one thing, only to leave you wanting when it's exposed for its empty promises. Mimicry never satisfies and it made me wonder, *How often does our enemy use mimicry to lure us into settling for a fake version of the real thing God is offering?*

Isaiah asks the question I sometimes ask myself, "Why spend money on what is not bread, and your labour on what does not satisfy?" (Isaiah 55:2).

We all do it. We all "spend" ourselves pursuing peace, joy, love, hope, and so much more, in all manner of places, and often it's the fake version we're pursuing instead of the good, rich real deal that Jesus is offering. We settle for the mimic, and it never satisfies.

Friends, we need to stop looking to wealth, health, image, status, careers, sports, sex, family, or any number of things to satisfy us. At some point we find out the bread was never really bread, and we're left feeling hollow and hungry.

So often I have to remind myself of Isaiah's exhortation to consume that which satisfies, "Listen, listen to me, and eat what is good, and you will delight in the richest of fare" (Isaiah 55:2).

Only Jesus can satisfy. Only Jesus is the real deal. Only Jesus will bring you peace, hope, love, and joy in a way that endures no matter the circumstance or situation. Don't build your life pursuing fake substitutes. Don't be conned by the devil's schemes and mimicry. Demand truth, and then you shall have life to the full as you receive "the richest of fare" that God is waiting to give you.

WHY SPEND YOUR MONEY ON
SOMETHING THAT IS NOT REAL
FOOD? WHY WORK FOR SOMETHING
THAT DOESN'T REALLY SATISFY
YOU? LISTEN CLOSELY TO ME, AND
YOU WILL EAT WHAT IS GOOD.
YOU WILL ENJOY THE FOOD THAT
SATISFIES YOUR SOUL.

ISAIAH 55:2 ICB

Father, I want the real deal. I won't settle for anything less than the best that Jesus has for me. He is the One that I will spend my life for. I am satisfied by His peace, joy, hope, and love.

The Soil of Fruitfulness

AIMÉE

By nature, I am an independent person, tending towards pushing ahead and getting things done by relying on my own capabilities and resources. Jesus constantly has to remind me that apart from Him, I can do nothing (John 15:5).

Nothing. Not some things. *Nothing.*

Nothing of eternal value; nothing that truly matters can be achieved independent of Jesus. A life of mature fruitfulness can only grow out of being fully dependent on Him.

The dictionary describes dependence as 'the state of relying on or needing someone or something for aid, support, or the like'. It can be a humbling thing, a terrifying thing even, to be faced with the inadequacies of our own resources and abilities. But it can also be a beautiful thing.

Twelve times in John 15, Jesus uses the words 'abide' or 'remain', commanding us to abide in Him and in His love, and to allow Him and His Word to abide in us. The word used here means 'to sojourn or tarry; not to depart but to be held, kept, continually; to remain as one, not to become another or different, to wait'. Dependence is not a restriction upon us, but an invitation to intimacy—an invitation to linger in His presence and allow Him to keep and sustain us. And if we do this, He promises us we will bear much fruit. Independence is the ground of barrenness but dependence is the soil of fruitfulness.

When I find myself grinding to a halt and all my efforts seem futile; when I find myself feeling spent and empty and my joy is lacking, I have to ask myself this simple question: *Am I abiding in Christ?* If the answer is no, then it's time for a reset.

We have the opportunity each and every day to begin again—to choose to navigate the day with Jesus not only beside us, but leading us. Today, take a moment to linger in His presence and wait for His instruction. Allow Him to order your priorities and trust Him to grow something beautiful in your life as you embrace the simplicity of abiding.

I AM THE VINE; YOU ARE THE BRANCHES. IF YOU REMAIN IN ME AND I IN YOU, YOU WILL BEAR MUCH FRUIT; APART FROM ME YOU CAN DO NOTHING.

JOHN 15:5

Father, I acknowledge that apart from Jesus I can do nothing. I accept Your invitation of intimacy and I choose today to abide and linger in Your presence. I want to bear much fruit and I will depend on You alone to bring that fruit forth.

Say the Things

EMILY

When my daughter was four years old we would occasionally whisper to her at bedtime. We would whisper truth and affirmation, encouragement and hope. We would whisper things like, "You are kind... you are brave... you are a daughter of the King... you are a joy-bringer..."

One evening I began to leave the room *before* whispering.

"Say the things Mummy. Say the things."

My darling girl found peace and was able to drift off to sleep when she was in the presence of her parents who loved her enough to declare who she was. She found hope for the unknown, confidence for the following day, and comfort that she was fully known, accepted, and loved. As she's grown, it's still the thing she desires most at bedtime. To be affirmed and reminded of who she is.

My husband and I aren't genius parents. We copied this idea from One who has been whispering truth long before we ever thought to:

"You are chosen... you are not a mistake... you are fearfully and wonderfully made... it is my desire to lavish my love on you... you are my treasured possession... you are a new creation... you are a child of God... you are in Christ!" (Ephesians 1:11-12; Psalm 139:14-16; 1 John 3:1; Exodus 19:5; 2 Corinthians 5:17; John 1:12; Romans 8:1).

In Christ you are fruitful, accepted, and forgiven. In Christ you are strengthened, an overcomer, and included. In Christ you are called a child of God, royal, and friend. In Christ you are beloved, safely hidden, and secure. In Christ you are loved, called, given purpose. In Christ you are salt, light, and good news.

Your Heavenly Father isn't just whispering these declarations of love over you. He's taking great delight in you and rejoicing over you with singing. This week, call out to your Heavenly Daddy to "say the things," and then take some time to listen to His song.

THE LORD YOUR GOD IS WITH YOU,
THE MIGHTY WARRIOR WHO SAVES.
HE WILL TAKE GREAT DELIGHT
IN YOU; IN HIS LOVE HE WILL NO
LONGER REBUKE YOU, BUT WILL
REJOICE OVER YOU WITH SINGING.

ZEPHANIAH 3:17

Father, I choose to listen to the things You
speak over me and to me. I will delight in Your
love and affirmation, and silence any voice
that doesn't align with what You have to say.

Change Your Clothes

AIMÉE

We started off married-life as two green kids still at university and knee deep in student debt—debt that because of our lack of wisdom would keep growing until we buckled beneath its weight.

It was a season of our lives that we didn't steward well; a season that the consequences have long out-lasted.

It was a season that, for better or worse, I allowed to define me; to label me a failure and a burden and clothe me in shame.

When I was growing up, my dad always had a favourite track-suit that he would change into when he got home from work—his 'second skin' we called it. He was so reluctant to part with these items of clothing that he would wear them until they were falling apart. One such tracksuit, threadbare and paint-stained, drove my mother to desperate measures, and under the guise of cutting off a loose thread, she cut the jumper from top to bottom—while he was wearing it! I'll never forget the look on his face as it fell off him or how he made her sew it back up so he could keep wearing it.

How often do we insist on continuing to wear the filthy rags that Jesus has cut off us?

In Ephesians 4:22-24, Paul instructs us to put off our old self and to put on the new self that is created to be like God in true righteousness and holiness. The truth is, in Christ we are a new creation—the old has gone and the new has come (2 Corinthians 5:17). We have been made right with God and we need to deliberately take off the lies that we've absorbed and put on that truth.

My own journey has taught me that while we might have to live with the consequences of our actions and decisions—of the 'old'—we need not live with any condemnation. No matter how comfortable we are in what we have always known, the garments God wants to clothe us in are a much better fit. So now, the only labels I will wear are the ones He has fashioned for me.

What do you need to take off today, and what is God inviting you to put on instead?

...PUT OFF YOUR OLD SELF, WHICH IS BEING CORRUPTED BY ITS DECEITFUL DESIRES; TO BE MADE NEW IN THE ATTITUDE OF YOUR MINDS; AND TO PUT ON THE NEW SELF, CREATED TO BE LIKE GOD IN TRUE RIGHTEOUSNESS AND HOLINESS.

EPHESIANS 4:22B-24

Father, thank You that there is no condemnation for those who are in Christ. I believe You have removed my sin and my shame from me and that I am now a new creation. I refuse to let my past define me, Christ alone now has that authority.

Under Pressure

EMILY

Pressure can be a good thing. I know this to be true because, right now, the pressure applied to my finger has stopped the bleeding caused by slicing it open on the metal hob extractor. *The lesson?* Don't clean.

Seriously though, without pressure, caterpillars wouldn't transform into butterflies, wounds wouldn't close, diamonds wouldn't form, babies wouldn't be pushed through the birth canal, the garden path wouldn't get clean, and the meat wouldn't become half as tender in your casserole.

We need pressure in our lives.

However, we tend to avoid it, as no one likes the idea of being constrained or even crushed because of pressure. We say things like, "she's under too much pressure," and advise others to lessen their workload so that the pressure doesn't cause them to buckle under the strain. Self-preservation at all costs! James has a different way of looking at it:

> "Consider it a sheer gift, friends, when tests and challenges come at you from all sides. You know that under pressure, your faith-life is forced into the open and shows its true colours" (James 1:2-3 MSG).

Countless tasks, financial strain, extreme workloads, tense relationships. . . *consider it all a gift?* I'm not so sure about that! But I do know that when I took the pressure off my finger too soon, the blood kept flowing. It was an object lesson in James' caution: "So don't try and get out of anything prematurely. Let it do its work" (James 1:4 MSG). Even though it might not feel very nice at the time, that pressure is doing an important job.

Pressure compels us to examine what's important in any given moment. It focuses us and forces out of us what's really inside. If you're feeling under pressure at the moment, don't run from it, instead allow it to propel you towards Jesus. Ask God to meet you in the pressure and use it to make you "mature and well-developed, not deficient in any way" (James 1:4 MSG). Your faith is more precious than gold, and we all know gold must endure a furnace in order to come out pure.

Pressure can be a good thing. Embrace it.

YOU KNOW THAT THESE THINGS
ARE TESTING YOUR FAITH. AND THIS
WILL GIVE YOU PATIENCE. LET YOUR
PATIENCE SHOW ITSELF PERFECTLY
IN WHAT YOU DO. THEN YOU WILL
BE PERFECT AND COMPLETE. YOU
WILL HAVE EVERYTHING YOU NEED.

JAMES 1:3-4 ICB

Father, I choose today to see the pressure in
my life as a gift. When I'm tempted to short-
cut the process and run from demanding
situations, I will remember that my faith is
precious and that You are able to use these
things to bring me to maturity in Christ.

What Do You Hear?

AIMÉE

It had been a long dry summer that had stretched into autumn, and our water tank had been continually bordering on empty. My heart felt just as empty and I found myself echoing the cry of David: "I spread out my hands to you; my soul thirsts for you like a parched land" (Psalm 143:6).

I take comfort in knowing that the Scriptures are full of men and women who experienced 'dry' seasons. Elijah was one of them. In 1 Kings, we're told he experienced periods of both drought and depression. On one such occasion, Israel had no rain—not even dew—for three whole years. The brooks dried up, resources were scarce, and the people were struggling. Yet Elijah went to King Ahab and made this declaration: "Go, eat and drink, for there is the sound of a heavy rain" (1 Kings 18:41).

There was not a cloud in the sky at the time he spoke these words. Elijah heard prophetically—he heard the answer, the promise of God in relation to their need before it was a visible reality. But it's what he did next that caused the sound of rain to become the release of rain. Elijah climbed to the top of Mt. Carmel, bent down to the ground, and put his face between his knees (18:42)—he chose to align himself with what God was saying and to then persevere in prayer.

In Hebrew, *Carmel* means 'a garden land; a place of fruitfulness or fertility'. In a time of need and lack, Elijah chose to retreat to a place of fruitfulness. Prayer—our intimate communion with the Father—is that place. And it is where Elijah stayed until he saw the clouds of rain beginning to rise from the sea; until what he had heard in his spirit was made manifest in the physical realm.

As I spread out my needs before God, He whispered three words to me: *On your knees*. God wants to release the rains of His Spirit to quench parched hearts and lands, and He wants us to be part of releasing that rain. So He is calling us back to the fruitful place—back to our knees, back to intimacy.

What do you hear today? Will you partner with Him to make it seen?

SO COME, LET US WORSHIP: BOW BEFORE HIM, ON YOUR KNEES BEFORE GOD, WHO MADE US! OH YES, HE'S OUR GOD, AND WE'RE THE PEOPLE HE PASTURES, THE FLOCK HE FEEDS. DROP EVERYTHING AND LISTEN, LISTEN AS HE SPEAKS.

PSALM 95:6–7 MSG

Father, I kneel before You today, drawing near in humble dependence to listen to what You have to say. I commit to be faithful in prayer—to cultivate the 'fruitful place' that I might partner with You to release the resources of Heaven in this season.

Low Ground

EMILY

A local school's slogan reads: "Empowered, confident, humble. Ready." Empowered, yes. Confident, yes. Ready, yes. . . *but humble?* We lift up the go-getters, the pioneers, the self-made entrepreneurs, but it's not often that humility is celebrated in our society.

Humility can be understood to mean that someone is insignificant or naïve. But it isn't weakness; it isn't lack of skill or talent. Humility begins with a correct understanding of our strengths, influence, and capabilities—and only from that place of power are we able to lower ourselves in order to elevate, celebrate, or serve another. The best example of humility was when God chose to come to earth in human form and was obedient to the point of death on a cross (Philippians 2:8). *When Jesus chose to follow through on that ruthless rescue, was He displaying weakness, insignificance, or naivety?* No. He was not.

The word 'humility' finds its roots in the Latin *humus* which means 'ground' and *humilis* which means 'low' or 'lowly'. It's the gritty, dirty earthen base that true humility comes from. And that's where we started too. God "remembers that we are dust" (Psalm 103:14 ESV). Yet "the Lord your God has chosen you to be his own special treasure. [He] did not set his heart on you and choose you because you were more numerous than other nations, for you were the smallest of all nations! Rather, it was simply that the Lord loves you. . . " (Deuteronomy 7:6-8 NLT).

You are chosen. You are special. You are loved.

What stops us from being humble then, is a misunderstanding of who we truly are. We find ourselves unable to lower ourselves when we seek to find our worth in position, power, or the perception of others. Stuck believing that we're only dirt, we strive to gain significance from something that is irrelevant compared to who we are in Christ: Chosen. Special. Loved.

Only when we remember who we truly are—whose we truly are—can we clothe ourselves with humility and serve one another in love. So yes, as Christians, let's be empowered by Holy Spirit, confident in the knowledge of the love of God, and humble like Jesus so that we might be ready to go into all the world. I guess it's not such a bad motto after all.

FOR HE KNOWS OUR FRAME; HE REMEMBERS THAT WE ARE DUST.

PSALM 103:14 ESV

Father, in humility I remember that You are God, and I am not, and I stand in awe of the lengths that You went to to rescue and redeem me. Today I hold my head high, knowing that, in Christ, I am loved and equipped for all things. In Your strength, I will love and serve willingly.

Stepping into Moses' Shoes

AIMÉE

Intimidated: 'to feel frightened or nervous in a situation because you are not confident in a situation; to lack confidence or be filled with fear'.

Honestly, most days as I scroll through my Social Media feeds, I feel the weight of intimidation in some form. Everyone else feels like a better mum, a better wife, a better homemaker, a better writer, a better. . . Comparison tempts me to doubt my abilities and contributions in this season and sometimes even causes me to shrink back.

I sometimes wonder if Joshua felt this way when he stepped into Moses' shoes. I mean, imagine taking over from the guy who'd led Israel out of slavery into freedom, and talked to God face-to-face—talk about intimidating!

God must have known the thoughts and fears swirling around in Joshua's mind, because as He commands Joshua to get ready to cross over into their promised land, He affirms His promises to Israel and repeatedly reminds Joshua that His presence will be with him to enable him to complete the task. "Have I not commanded you?" He says to Joshua. "Be strong and courageous. Do not be afraid; do not be discouraged, for the Lord your God will be with you wherever you go" (Joshua 1:9).

Joshua was not invited to be strong and courageous because of his own abilities, but God's. We, too, are called to live our lives in light of the truth that God Himself is with us.

If Joshua had been focused on comparing himself to Moses, I very much doubt Israel would have broken camp that day; wilderness living would have continued to be their experience. But because Joshua chose to be obedient to what God was asking him to do and be, following where and as He led, an entire nation possessed what had been promised to them.

Where has intimidation or comparison been holding you back from what God has placed in your heart to do and be? Today, He invites you to stop being paralysed by watching the life that others are living and to boldly and obediently live your own life well, encouraged by His promises and empowered by His presence.

. . .LET'S JUST GO AHEAD AND BE WHAT WE WERE MADE TO BE, WITHOUT ENVIOUSLY OR PRIDEFULLY COMPARING OURSELVES WITH EACH OTHER, OR TRYING TO BE SOMETHING WE AREN'T.

ROMANS 12:6A MSG

Father, I will be strong and courageous and do the work that You have for me to do. I know that You are always with me and will empower me for all that You call me to. I believe that my obedience has the power to bring breakthrough to others because You are mighty within me.

Strong and Steady

EMILY

My children have particular routines and structures that they like to keep. They listen to the same song at bedtime every night, followed by prayers—"you first, then me." The teddy needs to be wrapped in a specific blanket in a particular way. If you try to change their bedtime routine, drive home a different way from the shops, or serve food that is touching other food on the plate—you will certainly know about it! I have learned by now not to upset the status quo!

Routine and structure appear in our lives from a young age. Knowing what to expect is reassuring and makes us feel safe. It's the same for us as adults. We don't like change either. Familiarity and predictability bolsters our confidence and makes us feel that everything is alright in the world.

However, we've all lived through at least one season of extreme unpredictability and change. During the Covid-19 pandemic, changes happened so fast—not even day-by-day, but often hour-by-hour. Borders were closed, jobs were lost, finances were tight, sport fixtures were cancelled, and retirement villages were in lockdown preventing visitors from entering.

Change can be overwhelming, confusing, and when unknown viruses are added to the mix, change can be panic-inducing. *So what are we to do?*

In the midst of all the change, we need an anchor to ground us and a hope to steady us. How good it is that we can "say with confidence, 'The Lord is my helper; I will not be afraid. What can mere mortals do to me?' . . . Jesus Christ is the same yesterday and today and forever" (Hebrews 13:6, 8).

We have, in Jesus, a never-changing God who rules over all. A God who is not surprised by fast-changing global events, who never misses a beat nor looks the other way. We have, in Jesus, a God who is strong enough and steady enough for us to lean into when everything else around us seems to be changing. He is our ever-stable constant and anchors us in the storms we face. He is our safe and powerful place to find refuge.

Hold fast to the anchor in the storm. Hold fast to the hope in the change.

GOD IS A SAFE PLACE TO HIDE,
READY TO HELP WHEN WE NEED HIM.
WE STAND FEARLESS AT THE CLIFF-
EDGE OF DOOM, COURAGEOUS IN
SEASTORM AND EARTHQUAKE."

PSALM 46:1-2 MSG

Father, I cling to Jesus, my anchor, when life is tumultuous and unexpected. In Him I find safety and rest, ready help in my times of need. I am courageous, because I am secure in Your love and You are the same today, yesterday, and forever.

Your True Name

AIMÉE

I grew up constantly correcting how people spelt and pronounced my surname, so despite my pride in being a 'Kefali', I was quite happy to trade it in for my husband's plain and simple, 'Walker'. No more spelling my name out letter by letter over the phone! Yet even though I no longer carry the name Kefali, it still forms an important part of my identity and my sense of belonging—that's the power of names.

Sadly though, we often carry names and labels that we were never intended to carry.

Failure
Unwanted
Trouble
Burden
Useless

Sometimes we've assigned these names to ourselves, other times people have placed them on us. But these labels are not our true identity, for in Christ, we have been given a name that eclipses all others; we bear the Father's name.

In Ephesians 3:14-15, as Paul prays for the Church, he says this: "For this reason I fall on my knees before the Father, from whom every family in heaven and on earth receives its true name" (GNT).

If God had a surname—and we knew what it was—it would also be ours. Just like when I said, "I do" all those years ago and took my husband's name, when we say "yes" to Jesus, God gives us His family name. Whatever other names this life has attached to us, this name tells us that we belong, that we are loved, that we are His. It is our true name and our true identity.

So today, don't let yourself be defined by any name but His. Walk in the truth that God has redeemed you and called you by name (Isaiah 43:1), and allow the name that you now bear to speak to you of your value and worth; let it remind you that you are so very precious and loved.

I WILL WRITE ON THEM THE NAME OF MY GOD AND THE NAME OF THE CITY OF MY GOD, THE NEW JERUSALEM, WHICH IS COMING DOWN OUT OF HEAVEN FROM MY GOD; AND I WILL ALSO WRITE ON THEM MY NEW NAME.

REVELATION 3:12B

Father, I thank You for the honour of belonging to Your family and bearing Your name. I reject the names and labels that do not align with my true identity as a beloved child of God and instead choose to walk confidently in the truth of who I am in You.

Our Insurance Policy

EMILY

No one likes the idea of the unknown: medical bills we can't afford, homes ravaged by natural disasters, loved ones left in the lurch unprovided for. So, we take out insurance. We consider the risk and think of ways to mitigate the loss or damage.

Neil Armstrong and the Apollo 11 crew understandably had some trouble finding an insurance company that would underwrite their trip to the moon. Facing the possibility that they wouldn't return, the team signed hundreds of autographs and left them with their families, so the autographs could be sold in case the crew didn't return from their mission.

Life is full of risk.

Isaiah writes about the "scoffers" who say, "We've taken out good life insurance. We've hedged all our bets, covered all our bases. No disaster can touch us. We've thought of everything. We're advised by the experts. We're set" (Isaiah 28:15 MSG). Our natural inclination as humans is to do this. To take matters into our own hands, sign all the bits of paper we can find, consider all possible outcomes, and then put insurance in place to feel like we have control over the unplanned things.

But the reality is there's nothing that we can do to insure ourselves against the inevitable pain, loss, and challenge that life brings. We are not in control, and no amount of money can save us. Our value and safety isn't in what we can do. It's never enough. "No one can redeem the life of another or give to God a ransom for them—the ransom for a life is costly, no payment is ever enough" (Psalm 49:7-8).

But there is good news. God laid down a "precious cornerstone" that "the one who relies on it will never be stricken with panic" (Isaiah 28:16). We can be free from the fear of the unknown and 'what ifs' because Jesus is our assurance, insurance, and guarantee.

He's the policy you need to hold onto.

"LOOK! I AM PLACING A FOUNDATION STONE IN JERUSALEM, A FIRM AND TESTED STONE. IT IS A PRECIOUS CORNERSTONE THAT IS SAFE TO BUILD ON. WHOEVER BELIEVES NEED NEVER BE SHAKEN."

ISAIAH 28:16B NLT

Father, I will not fear the unknown or panic about what I cannot control. Jesus, You are my firm foundation—tried, tested, and enduring forever, You are my guarantee of what is to come. I build my life on You.

Stand Your Ground

AIMÉE

In this season of my life, cleaning often invites profound God conversations. As I tidy and sort, picking up the trail of chaos that follows my creative children, I find God organising and rearranging the messy, tangled places of my own heart.

I was wiping sticky prints off walls one day, wishing I could wipe away a challenging situation just as easily, when I felt Him ask me, "Have you done all that you can do?" "Yes!" I replied. "Then now is the time to stand firm and see what only *I* can do."

In Ephesians 6:13, Paul instructs us to put on the *full* armour of God so that we can stand our ground against the enemy. He then goes on to say, ". . . and having done everything, to stand."

We are co-labourers with God. We have a role to play. And in the situations and battles that we face, there are some things that are *our* responsibility. But after that—after we have done everything that we can to meet that deadline; to train our children in the way that they should go; to repair that relationship, then it is time to stand firm in what only *He* can do. It's time to clothe ourselves in His power and in the truth of who *He* is.

The armour we've been given is not just any armour, it's God's armour (Ephesians 6:11 & 13)— it's what He is depicted wearing when He goes into battle (Isaiah 59). We can stand firm, therefore, when the battle rages around us because of the divine nature of the weapons we've been given to fight with. Each piece of armour that Paul describes also represents an aspect of who Christ is. As we put it on, we remember that He is *the* truth; that He has become our righteousness; that He is the Prince of Peace—we gain the strength we need by 'putting on' Christ, leaning into all that He is and all that He has done. Wearing the armour is about allowing ourselves to be clothed in His abilities, not our own.

So today, where your efforts end and where you have done all that you know to do, stand your ground in that place, allowing His grace to cover you. Rest in His power and faithfulness, and then wait with expectation for what only God can do.

HE SAYS, "BE STILL, AND KNOW THAT I AM GOD; I WILL BE EXALTED AMONG THE NATIONS, I WILL BE EXALTED IN THE EARTH." THE LORD ALMIGHTY IS WITH US; THE GOD OF JACOB IS OUR FORTRESS.

PSALM 46:10-11

Father, I stand firm today in the truth of who You are, arming myself with Your strength and Your power. I know that the outcome of the battle lies not in my ability, but in Christ's. I trust that You will be exalted in my life and I still myself before You.

Don't Hold Back

EMILY

Forgive me all you green fingered genii. . . this isn't my forte, but I've been considering seeds and the idea of potting up. *Why do we plant seeds in little pots in the first place?* Essentially, to look after them in their fragile and immature state. A seedling needs to be nurtured and cared for so that it gets just the right amount of moisture, the right amount of space, and avoids being crowded by other plants and roots.

However, there comes a time when the seed needs to be repotted. The seed needs a larger growing space because if left in its small pot, the roots would become crowded and compacted. Without enough space, the plant would experience stunted growth. It wouldn't reach its full potential. And, it could even die.

Isaiah 54:2 says, "Enlarge the place of your tent, stretch your tent curtains wide, do not hold back; lengthen your cords, strengthen your stakes."

People were not made for isolation. We were not made for separation. Rather, we were made for growth, for enlarging, for expansion, for community, and intimacy. For many it felt scary to re-enter the world after a season of enforced lockdown during the COVID-19 pandemic. Similarly it's possible to feel anxious about expanding your horizons and seeing other people again after loss or other significant life changes.

But, I urge you, in spite of how you may feel, do not hold back.

Do not hold back from people. Do not hold back from sharing your lives. Do not hold back from allowing God to re-pot you into a new and more expansive place. As the psalmist writes, "He brought me out into a spacious place; he rescued me because he delighted in me" (Psalm 18:19). God is in the business of continually 'potting up' his people. He doesn't want you to remain stagnant and squashed.

So even if it feels scary or awkward; even if it means you have to step outside that which feels comfortable, don't hold back. Go and enlarge your pot bit by bit knowing that He desires growth for you and brings you to a spacious place because He delights in you!

"ENLARGE THE PLACE OF YOUR
TENT, STRETCH YOUR TENT
CURTAINS WIDE, DO NOT HOLD
BACK: LENGTHEN YOUR CORDS,
STRENGTHEN YOUR STAKES."

ISAIAH 54:2

Father, today, I will not hold back. I am Your
delight and I will walk in pleasant and wide
places. I expand the boundaries in my life
to allow for Your increase and blessing.

Make God Your Stronghold

AIMÉE

As a young woman, I committed the opening verses of Psalm 18 to memory:

"I love You, O Lord, my strength.
The Lord is my rock, my fortress and my deliverer;
my God is my rock, in whom I take refuge.
He is my shield and the horn of my salvation, my stronghold.
I call to the Lord who is worthy of praise,
and I am saved from my enemies."

Something deep within me was drawn to these verses. David's words captured my heart and reminded me that not only was God all these incredible things—strong, a rock, a fortress, a deliverer, a refuge, a shield, and a stronghold—He was these things *for me*. He was *my* strength, *my* rock, and *my* fortress.

However, it wasn't until years later that the word 'stronghold' really caught my attention. I had always thought of strongholds in a somewhat negative light, understanding them to be something that needed to be torn down and dismantled because it was enemy territory—an area of my life that he had gained control of. But if that was the case, *How could God possibly be my stronghold?*

The dictionary defines a stronghold as a place that has been fortified so as to protect it against attack or a place where a particular cause or belief is strongly defended or upheld. *What if instead of tearing down strongholds, we're meant to be focused more on building them? On being so utterly convinced of God's goodness, so deeply in love with who He is, that He, and not the enemy, becomes the stronghold of our lives?*

In life, there are so many things that seek to dethrone God from His rightful place at the centre of our hearts. We must be intentional about protecting and cultivating our intimacy with Him, because when we make our relationship with God the impenetrable place in our hearts, no matter what life throws at us, we will not be shaken. Circumstances will not be able to erode the truth of who He is and the strongholds of the enemy will inevitably crumble as we stand confident in faith.

THE LORD IS MY LIGHT AND MY SALVATION–WHOM SHALL I FEAR? THE LORD IS THE STRONGHOLD OF MY LIFE–OF WHOM SHALL I BE AFRAID?

PSALM 27:1

Father, I worship You today. You are my strength, my rock, my fortress, and my deliverer. I commit to make You my stronghold—to cultivate and guard our intimacy so that You are the impenetrable place in my heart.

No Messy Tail for You

EMILY

A couple of years ago, we were fortunate enough to stay at a sheep and cattle station. We stayed during docking season and were invited to go and watch the process.

Docking is the shortening of a lamb's tail and there are a variety of ways a farmer might do this. One method places a tight ring around the tail which cuts off circulation. When the dead part falls off, the lamb is left with a shorter tail. Suffice to say, it seemed rather intrusive and unpleasant for the lamb.

The problem is, if you don't dock a lamb's tail, the lamb is unable to clean itself which leads to a wide variety of diseases and other complications. What seems painful in the moment is actually necessary for a healthy and fruitful life.

Jesus told us to do something similar, "If your right eye causes you to stumble, gouge it out and throw it away. . . if your right hand causes you to stumble, cut it off and throw it away" (Matthew 5:29-30).

It may seem like a pretty intense and harsh directive, but Jesus wants us to understand the severity of what will happen if we insist on carrying temptation and sin around with us. If we don't make a decisive effort to remove the 'long tails', it can lead to filth and disease in our lives. Paul exhorts the Colossians in a similar manner, "Put to death. . . rid yourselves. . ." (Colossians 3:5-10). In other words, stick a tight ring on it, let it die, and fall away from you! What might seem drastic in the short term may ultimately save you from getting caught up in all sorts of mess and nastiness later.

However, don't despair. Just as a lamb isn't expected to dock its tail alone, neither does God expect us to deal with our temptation and sin independently. He promises "a way out" so we can endure temptation (1 Corinthians 10:13), and He is always "faithful and just" when we confess before Him. Not only will He forgive our sins, but He'll purify us too (1 John 1:9).

No messy tail for you.

YOU'RE DONE WITH THAT OLD
LIFE. IT'S LIKE A FILTHY SET OF
ILL-FITTING CLOTHES YOU'VE
STRIPPED OFF AND PUT IN THE
FIRE. NOW YOU'RE DRESSED IN A
NEW WARDROBE.

COLOSSIANS 3:9-10 MSG

Father, You take sin seriously and I will too; I will
not allow this new life You have given me to be
infected by it. With Your help, I rid myself of it,
stripping it off like a filthy garment and gratefully
receiving the clothes Christ has made me.

Fear Not

AIMÉE

We were on the other side of what had been an enormously stressful two years fostering our young nephew and raising our own preschoolers while my husband was unemployed. Our circumstances had begun to shift, but physically and emotionally I was spent. After years of pouring myself out and trying to ease my nephew's anxieties, I, too, now found myself gripped with anxiety. And I was so afraid. Afraid of going back to what had been. Afraid of what the future might hold. Still young in years, I felt weary and somewhat cynical on the inside.

Longing to experience the freedom that Christ promises, I set out to study all the references in Scripture in relation to fear. While I didn't make it through all of them, my study left me with a profound revelation: My fear was an invitation to worship.

The word 'fear' often gets a bad rap. In our desire to be obedient to Scripture's frequent command to "fear not," we can inadvertently buy into the idea that we are being asked to be fearless, when actually what we are being called to do is to rightly position our fear. The word most commonly translated as 'fear' in the New Testament, is a Greek word, *phobeō*. It can mean 'to be afraid, to put to flight by terrifying, to fear or be startled'. But it can also mean 'to be struck with amazement or to reverence, venerate, to treat with deference or reverential obedience'. Like a two-sided coin, *phobeō* presents us with a choice: *Will our fears terrify and shut us down, or will they lead us closer to God?*

It is not realistic to think that this world will never strike fear within us. Every day offers up plenty of reasons for us to be afraid. And God knew this—that's why the commands He gives us to "fear not" are always followed with a promise—a promise of His love, or His mighty power, or His presence. When God asks us to fear not, He is not trying to tell us that our circumstances are not daunting, rather He is inviting us to change our focus and to see how He walks through them *with* us.

Where do you need to allow your fear to lead you into deeper worship?

HAVE I NOT COMMANDED YOU?
BE STRONG AND COURAGEOUS.
DO NOT BE AFRAID; DO NOT BE
DISCOURAGED, FOR THE LORD
YOUR GOD WILL BE WITH YOU
WHEREVER YOU GO.

JOSHUA 1:9

Father, I choose today to let my fear draw me closer
to You. I will magnify You and let You be bigger than
the things that I face; I know that You are with me
and will be faithful to all that You have promised.

Oily and Anointed

EMILY

When I finished high school, I was given the school technology prize. I was rarely happier in school than when I was behind a decent power tool. Looking back, I remember how often the solution to a materials-based problem would be "WD-40." *Squeaky hinges?* WD-40. *Rust?* WD-40. *Paint removal?* WD-40.

It turns out that even as an adult, WD-40 continues to be a solution for any number of problems: removing rust, loosening bolts, removing bird poop from your car, cleaning, polishing, preventing dirt from sticking to your mountain bike, keeping bugs at bay in the house, removing crayon from walls, unsticking piano keys, stopping wasps from nesting... *Got a problem?* The answer is probably WD-40.

You see, if things are stuck, rusting, or wedged then you usually need a good lubricant to get it moving again. You need to minimise friction if you want to have a smoother process and forward momentum. If you want to clean something without damaging the material underneath, a good lubricant can loosen the grime and free the surface from lasting damage or disfigurement. If you want to avoid dirt or pests from setting up home, you need an impenetrable barrier.

Sometimes in life we get a bit creaky. Things seize up and stop functioning as they should. Maybe we have rusty relationships. Perhaps, like a car parked under a tree, someone else has come along and dumped all their mess on top of us. Possibly our devotion to God has dulled and needs a polish. Or maybe we need a repellent for the sinful snares that seek to steal us away from deeper intimacy with Jesus.

Our lives need lubrication, and throughout Scripture, Holy Spirit is likened to oil. "You have been anointed by the Holy One... [and] the anointing that you received from him abides in you" (1 John 2:20, 27 ESV).

If you've been feeling stuck recently, I'm going to suggest you need a good drenching of oil. For if you "abide in" and are "filled with the Holy Spirit," (Ephesians 5:18 ESV), He can help you in your weakness. Before long, you will find yourself moving forward again, walking in freedom—rejuvenated, cleansed, and rust-free.

BUT THE ANOINTING THAT YOU
RECEIVED FROM HIM ABIDES IN
YOU, AND YOU HAVE NO NEED THAT
ANYONE SHOULD TEACH YOU. BUT
AS HIS ANOINTING TEACHES YOU
ABOUT EVERYTHING, AND IS TRUE,
AND IS NO LIE—JUST AS IT HAS
TAUGHT YOU, ABIDE IN HIM.

I JOHN 2:27 ESV

Father, in You, my weakness becomes strength. I
will move forward with confidence knowing I am
anointed with the oil of Your Spirit. I walk in freedom
as He guides, teaches, and leads me in Your truth.

The Proper Time

AIMÉE

It was a transitional season filled with significant delays. We had sensed God leading us to move, yet every attempt to make that move happen seemed to be opposed. We began to lose count of the houses we'd missed out on, and at times we wondered if we had heard Him right.

Yet I found myself anchored by a lesson God had taught me in another period of waiting. Throughout Scripture there are references to the 'proper time', the 'appointed time', the 'fullness of time', or the 'set time'. These phrases teach us that God not only has a plan, but He also has a timetable.

We often think about where we're going only in terms of how it affects us, but God's plans are Kingdom plans—He is weaving all our individual stories together to accomplish His plans for this point in *His*-story. Sometimes we are delayed because of what God needs to do in us, other times it may be related to what He is doing elsewhere. But whatever the reason, we can trust that God sees the complete picture and will bring everything to pass at just the right time—the proper time.

Psalm 145 gives us this encouragement for when we wait: "The eyes of all look to you, and you give them their food at the proper time. You open your hand and satisfy the desires of every living thing" (vv.15-16). God doesn't withhold things from us to frustrate us; His heart is to satisfy our desires with good things (Psalm 103). But for those desires to truly be the blessing He intends, they must be released and realised according to His timetable, not our own.

Our move did eventually happen, and when it did, the home God provided for us was above and beyond anything we had hoped for. It was a home that met the needs and desires of every single member of our family; a home that testified of His goodness and His faithfulness. As you wait on His timing in your own life, keep looking to Him, and be assured that His posture toward you is an open hand.

FOR THE REVELATION AWAITS AN
APPOINTED TIME; IT SPEAKS OF
THE END AND WILL NOT PROVE
FALSE. THOUGH IT LINGER, WAIT
FOR IT; IT WILL CERTAINLY COME
AND WILL NOT DELAY.

HABAKKUK 2:3

Father, I believe Your hand is open towards
me—that Your heart is to satisfy my desires with
good things. I yield my plans and my dreams to
You, trusting that at the proper time You will
bring what You have purposed for my life to pass.

Lifted Up

EMILY

"Mummy, Mummy, come and see." My daughter ran in from the garden, desperate to show us the soft pinky-peach sunset outside. She strained on her tiptoes but it had already sunk behind the fence and surrounding houses.

She knew there was beauty to behold but it was just out of reach. My husband swept her up and placed her high on his shoulders. Together they stood and took in the view, and with comfortable intimacy, enjoyed the ethereal exhibition.

Sometimes we experience life in a similar way. We know there is beauty to be encountered but it can seem just out of reach. We can't quite access it on our own. So, we strain on our tiptoes and strive to be holy enough to bask in the light. We might glimpse it, but our limitations and lack prohibit us from experiencing the full wonder and glory of all that God desires to bestow upon us. We don't have the power or strength to take hold of the blessing on offer.

Oftentimes in Scripture, when someone encounters God's glory they can do nothing but fall facedown (Ezekiel 43:3; Genesis 17:3; Numbers 14:5; 1 Chronicles 21:16). We are incapable of remaining upright in the presence of a holy and righteous God. And yet, time and again, in His great love for us, God comes down, lifts us up, sets us on our feet, and draws us into deeper intimacy so we can experience His glory *together* (Ezekiel 43:5). He desires for us to be raised up to be *with* Him.

Beautiful sunsets, sleeping babies, the metamorphosis of a butterfly—there are holy moments all around us, offering glimpses of a Heavenly Father who desires nothing more than to draw us into the inner court and share in the glory of His presence together.

Jesus came because God knows we are weak and small, incapable of getting there on our own. Instead of striving and straining, call out to Jesus and let Him lift you up to witness the wonder *with* Him.

THEN THE SPIRIT LIFTED ME UP
AND BROUGHT ME INTO THE INNER
COURT, AND THE GLORY OF THE
LORD FILLED THE TEMPLE.

EZEKIEL 43:5

Father, I bask in the wonder of Your
creation and relish being raised with You to
experience the fullness of Your goodness as
You reveal Yourself throughout my day. The
invitation to be in Your glorious presence
leaves me worshipping in wonder.

Chosen Strangers

AIMÉE

It was a season of momentous change for our family. Alongside starting to homeschool after many years in the public school system, and changing churches after some eighteen years, we had also moved to a new community. For the first time in a long while, I found myself the 'new girl'. I felt uncertain as to whether I really belonged in these new places, and many times I was unsure of where I 'fit'. Feeling somewhat of an outsider, I experienced a loneliness that was unfamiliar to me.

At the time, the introduction to Peter's first epistle deeply resonated with me: "To God's elect, strangers in the world. . . " (1 Peter 1:1). What stood out to me was these two seemingly opposed descriptions of who we are—both God's chosen ones *and* strangers in this world. The first speaks to me of belonging while the second makes me think of what it feels like to be displaced; to be on the outside looking in. *But what if they are both there to remind us that we are chosen, desired, and woven into a community?*

The word 'strangers' described someone who came from one country to live alongside the natives of another, and in the New Testament was used metaphorically to refer to Heaven as our country of origin. Its presence in this verse reminds us that when we feel like foreigners, it is because our place of true belonging is elsewhere—we belong to a Kingdom that transcends our knowledge. But it also reminds us that though this world is not our home, it *is* a place of purpose for us. For it is here that we have been commissioned to live alongside those whose hearts are set on what is temporal in order to point them to the wonder of what is eternal.

That season of feeling like a stranger in my own life, reminded me that when we feel like we are on the outside, we must stand firm in the truth that we are God's elect; handpicked by Him to be part of His family and to take our place in the unfolding of His great story.

Where is your heart set on belonging? Keep your eyes fixed on your true home and allow the light of eternity to bring hope and purpose to your days here.

BUT YOU ARE A CHOSEN PEOPLE, A ROYAL PRIESTHOOD, A HOLY NATION, GOD'S SPECIAL POSSESSION, THAT YOU MAY DECLARE THE PRAISES OF HIM WHO CALLED YOU OUT OF DARKNESS INTO HIS WONDERFUL LIGHT.

I PETER 2:9

Father, I thank You that I have a place of belonging that can never be taken away from me. I am Your chosen child and special possession, called and purposed to bring Your light and life to this world. I set my heart today on Your Kingdom, my true home.

Make Space

EMILY

A while back, one of our children was desperate to buy a nerf gun. It would take him more than ten weeks to save enough pocket money to buy the desired toy. Yet, only a little later, I was called to his bedroom. "I've made space. I've rearranged things. I'm getting ready..."

Sure enough, the underwear had been tipped out of its box to make space. Another drawer had been emptied. He was so eager that he'd made space for ammo in one box and had an entire drawer ready to house all the different types of nerf guns he was hoping for. My child was expectant. And His anticipation and hope led him to prepare for an abundance of toys.

Matthew 25 tells us of the parable of the ten virgins who were waiting to meet their Bridegroom. Half of them, in their anticipation and hope, prepared themselves and got ready. The other half, well, they couldn't be bothered. Maybe they didn't want to go out and buy the oil beforehand, maybe they didn't want to spend their money, maybe they didn't want to carry the extra oil from the outset—whatever the reason, they weren't prepared. They hadn't spent any time or energy investing in getting ready.

John the Baptist's entire ministry was calling people to "prepare the way for the Lord, make straight paths for him" (Mark 1:3). Calling us to repent, to prepare, to make space for the Lord in our hearts and in our lives.

How expectant are you to see God at work? To see Him answer prayer? To make a difference, change lives, set people free? Have you taken any time recently to prepare? Just as my child had to rearrange and reorder things to make space for what he was hoping for, we, too, need to reorder and make space for the Lord.

What things do you need to clear out of your life in order to make space for Jesus? Is there pride, unforgiveness, jealousy, anger, self-righteousness? This week, why not choose to intentionally "make space, rearrange things, get ready" to allow the Bridegroom to enter in and have His way with your heart, mind, finances, relationships, schedule, and life.

THE WISE ONES, HOWEVER, TOOK OIL IN JARS ALONG WITH THEIR LAMPS.

MATTHEW 25:4

Father, I stand expectant before You, ready to encounter You today. I let go of anything hindering communion with You and prepare my heart to make space for the blessings You have in store.

Joy Has a Sound

AIMÉE

From the moment our eyes open and our feet hit the floor we're generally surrounded by noise. Alarms, phones, radios, all manner of devices, voices, and sounds fill our hearts and minds throughout the course of the day. Some of these sounds are pleasant, soothing even. However, the reality is that much of the world's noise leaves us feeling harried and overwhelmed.

But have you ever realised that joy has a sound?

Time and again, the psalmists describe the jubilant sounds that creation makes as its celebrates its Creator, telling us how the rivers clap and the mountains sing (Psalm 98:8), how the meadows and valleys shout for joy and sing (Psalm 65:3), and the seas resound with praise (Psalm 96:11). Jesus even said that were His disciples to cease their praise, the very rocks would cry out (Luke 19:40). Creation cannot stay quiet. It must release the sound of the One that it adores.

Time and again, the psalmists exhort us to do likewise—to let our mouths open with songs of praise and cries of joy. We are to be a people who clap our hands and shout because we know how awesome our Lord is and we cannot keep it to ourselves (Psalm 47:1-2). Just as with creation, our lives were designed to resound with the sound of joy.

Yes, joy wasn't meant to be contained; it was intended to be heard. It is both a sound of celebration for life's beauty and a battle cry for its struggles. Because while we might not know all the details, we do know the end of the story. We know that God is with us and for us. We know that He's good and faithful. We know that He's able and powerful. We know that He's loving and gracious, and that He's returning.

We can rejoice in all that He is doing now and all that He is yet to do. So today, let the sound of our lives be joy in all that He is, and let that be the noise that we bring to this world.

GOD HAS ASCENDED AMID
SHOUTS OF JOY, THE LORD AMID
THE SOUNDING OF TRUMPETS. SING
PRAISES TO GOD, SING PRAISES;
SING PRAISES TO OUR KING, SING
PRAISES. FOR GOD IS THE KING OF
ALL THE EARTH; SING TO HIM A
PSALM OF PRAISE.

PSALM 47:5-7

Father, I will not stay quiet. I will sing and shout and
clap my hands and celebrate the greatness of who
You are. You are not only the King of all the earth,
You are my King and I want the world to know it!

Never Cut Off

EMILY

Tourniquets work by applying external pressure to limit (but not stop) the flow of blood. Despite their obvious advantages during a medical emergency, tourniquets can be dangerous. If you leave them in place for too long, irreparable muscle damage occurs which results in the eventual death of the muscle. A muscle cannot live without connection to the life source.

Paul warns of a similar situation in Galatians 5:4 in relation to our spiritual lives: "I suspect you would never intend this, but this is what happens. When you attempt to live by your own religious plans and projects, you are cut off from Christ, you fall out of grace" (MSG).

Sometimes we get so wrapped up in the 'stuff' of life that it entangles us and cuts off our connection to the Source of life—Jesus Christ. We never intend it, of course, but we fill our diaries; we fill our homes; we fill our minds. We busy ourselves and leave little room for Jesus to squeeze in. Perhaps we're filling our time with honourable and worthy pursuits, but the problem is, that when it becomes our everything and takes centre stage, it strangles our connection to Jesus leaving us haemorrhaging and barely functioning. We become cut off as distraction and activity reduces our intimacy with Jesus to barely a drip.

When your muscles don't receive enough blood they become starved of oxygen and symptoms of pain, aching, and numbness take over. I don't know about you, but as soon as I attempt to live life without Jesus as my Source, my pain, aching, and numbness increase. My life flow is squeezed so tightly that it's unsustainable.

Unlike a tourniquet, however, when this happens in our relationship with Jesus; when we have allowed the things of life to crush us, the damage is not irreparable. For "there is surely a future hope for you, and your hope will not be cut off" (Proverbs 23:18). Our hope cannot be cut off because Jesus endured and has overcome amputation from the Father on our behalf.

If you are feeling numb and struggling for oxygen, cry out to your Source of life: "I am cut off from your sight" (Psalm 31:22 ESV). He *will* hear your cry. In His mercy He will loosen the tourniquet's grip and its power over you, reinstating connection once again and restoring you to Himself and abundant, fully-functioning, free-flowing life.

THERE IS SURELY A FUTURE HOPE
FOR YOU, AND YOUR HOPE WILL
NOT BE CUT OFF.

PROVERBS 23:18

Father, thank You that no matter how distant
I may feel, I am never cut off from Your sight.
My hope is secure and Your presence assured.

Test Your Thoughts

AIMÉE

My mind can be a bit like a rabbit burrow—a series of intricate and complex underground tunnels hidden from the outside world. My thoughts run off on me, entertaining endless possibilities that will either burrow me down into deep, dark places or bring me up into the fresh open air and sunlight. I know which destination I prefer, but unfortunately I often allow myself to get lost in a labyrinth of dead ends and dark places that take me away from the peace and the quietness of soul that God desires me to know.

I regularly find myself drawn to the promise of Isaiah 26:3 where God tells us that, "[He] will keep in perfect peace all who trust in [Him], all whose thoughts are fixed on [Him]" (NLT). It reminds me that while it's God's job to do the keeping, it is my job to do the thinking. The quality of my thought life and the level of peace that I am experiencing are directly related.

Peace flows when we keep our minds, our thoughts fixed on the Prince of Peace, Jesus. In Philippians 4, Paul teaches us how to let Christ displace worry when he tells us to fill our minds with things that are true and noble, reputable and authentic, and so on.

These things that we are to fix our minds on are a practical way to test the health of our thoughts. We need to start asking ourselves: *Is this thought true? Is it right? Is it pure and lovely? Is it excellent and worthy of praise?* If it's not, then we need to tear it down and build a new thought. A thought that is centred on who God is—on His faithfulness, on His goodness, on His unfailing love. A thought that trusts in His wisdom and His purposes. A thought that stirs faith and hope; a thought that leads to a confident expectation of His goodness in my life and circumstances. A thought that is anchored in His Word and evidenced in the life and ministry of Jesus.

Where do you need to change your thinking and shift the focus to Jesus?

Let's make it a daily practice to be intentional with our thought life, bringing every wandering thought under His control (2 Corinthians 10:5) and giving Jesus space to rule and reign as the Prince of Peace.

AND NOW, DEAR BROTHERS AND
SISTERS, ONE FINAL THING. FIX
YOUR THOUGHTS ON WHAT IS
TRUE, AND HONOURABLE, AND
RIGHT, AND PURE, AND LOVELY,
AND ADMIRABLE. THINK ABOUT
THINGS THAT ARE EXCELLENT AND
WORTHY OF PRAISE.

PHILIPPIANS 4:8 NLT

Father, I submit my mind to You and take captive
the thoughts that do not align with the truth
of who You are. I will meditate on Your wonder
and think on that which is true and right and
worthy of praise. You keep me in perfect peace.

A Little While

EMILY

"How much longer will the pain last?" I sobbed to the doctor on the phone. I was dealing with bouts of recurring mastitis and thrush, and feeding my newborn was the most excruciating pain I had ever experienced. But I knew, *I knew*, that I would be able to press through the pain if I had the assurance it was only going to last a little while longer.

I've noticed that we often say unpleasant things will be over "in a little while": when a child needs a blood test, when the kids are wondering when a family walk will be over, visiting the dentist. It seems that we can often endure pain or suffering if we know it won't last forever.

Peter acknowledges that, "for a little while you may have had to suffer grief in all kinds of trials" (1 Peter 1:6), and Jesus Himself warned us we will have trouble in this world (John 16:33). But Jesus also used this phrase to reassure His disciples that He wouldn't be gone from them forever: "In a little while you will see me no more, and then after a little while you will see me" (John 16:16). He reassures us, too, that even though now may be our "time of grief" (v22), a time is coming when we will grieve no more and our grief will turn to joy (v20). A joy that no one can take away (v22).

A time is coming when "after you have suffered a little while, [God] will himself restore you and make you strong, firm and steadfast" (1 Peter 5:10). Unlike the disciples who had to endure time without Jesus, despite the trials and painful circumstances we might find ourselves in, our joy *can* be complete (John 16:24); Jesus has deposited His Holy Spirit in our hearts to "guide us into all truth" (v13).

No matter what challenge you find yourself facing, know that even if it feels like more than 'a little while', you have the Holy Spirit advocating for you, leading you, and guiding you in the middle of the pain. Call out to Jesus and allow Him to enter in. "For, 'In just a little while, he who is coming will come and will not delay'" (Hebrews 10:37). This pain will not last forever.

"I HAVE TOLD YOU THESE THINGS, SO THAT IN ME YOU MAY HAVE PEACE. IN THIS WORLD YOU WILL HAVE TROUBLE. BUT TAKE HEART! I HAVE OVERCOME THE WORLD."

JOHN 16:33

Father, I hold firm to Your promise of presence and peace in the midst of my circumstances. Holy Spirit will lead, guide, and advocate for me, and I will be restored, firm and steadfast as a result of Your hand on my life.

Make Your Bed

AIMÉE

I was sitting with my coffee cup in hand and my Bible on my knee, feeling overwhelmed by my to-do list, when God spoke to me. I wish I could tell you that in that moment I had been prayerfully seeking His guidance, but truthfully I had been procrastinating. Nonetheless, God spoke. He told me to go make my bed.

Confession: My bed seldom gets made. This is in part because I get up early and head straight to the kitchen for coffee upon waking, but mostly it's because in the scheme of running a household, it never quite makes it to the top of the list.

So that day, I headed upstairs and straightened my bed. It felt good. It brought a sense of order to the chaotic thoughts of my mind—and even a sense of accomplishment. If nothing else got completed that day, at least my bed had been made.

This little act of returning to making my bed has become a powerful, tangible reminder to me of Christ's words in Luke 16:10: "If you are faithful in little things, you will be faithful in large ones. . ." (NLT).

We often focus our time and attention on the 'big things'. We look at our end-goal and forget that the path there is usually made up of a million little steps. We forget that the things we aspire to be and possess are uncovered and realised little by little, moment by moment.

The little things don't always feel like the important things, and because of this, we can be tempted to overlook or rush through them, perhaps even skip them altogether. But Jesus cautions us that if we fail to steward what we already have, we will be unable to be entrusted not only with more, but also with true riches—the resources of Heaven (Luke 16:11).

Although they may not seem important, I've come to understand that the little things are actually big things. How we conduct ourselves in the unseen and often mundane places defines and shapes our lives. Our faithfulness in the little makes room for all that God intends for us to possess and experience.

What 'little' thing is God inviting you to pay attention to this week?

HIS MASTER REPLIED, "WELL DONE, GOOD AND FAITHFUL SERVANT! YOU HAVE BEEN FAITHFUL WITH A FEW THINGS; I WILL PUT YOU IN CHARGE OF MANY THINGS. COME AND SHARE YOUR MASTER'S HAPPINESS!"

MATTHEW 25:23

Father, I commit today to be a good steward of all that You have entrusted to me. I will not despise or overlook the 'little', but be faithful in it. I desire to be trusted with the riches of Heaven and to bring You joy and glory in both the seen and unseen.

Ready Access

EMILY

I once had a job where I needed a card to gain access to the building, use the lifts, enter the floor I worked on, get into particular meeting rooms, and even the toilet!

One morning, I arrived at work to find that my card had expired. I had to prove who I was to be accompanied to my office and could no longer freely enter any of the places I was used to accessing. What's more, that same day, the auto top-up for my bus pass failed and I was refused entry to the bus.

This double denial of access highlighted how much I took for granted these two small pieces of plastic that gave me freedom and access to go about my day. So often tossed to the bottom of my bag, they nonetheless held immense value in enabling me to live an unhindered life.

Jesus gives us "ready access" to God (Hebrews 4:14 MSG). He's made a way for us to walk in freedom, to "have complete and free access to God's kingdom, keys to open any and every door" (Matthew 16:19 MSG). *I wonder if we ever take the access Jesus won for us for granted?*

Jesus has provided us with access to God and His Kingdom that will never expire. With access, you enter a place with confidence knowing you belong; you walk in authority. In the same way, our prayers can be unhindered, reflecting the understanding that we have free access to the throne room to meet with the King of Kings, the Ruler of all, and that there are "no more barriers between heaven and earth" (Matthew 16:19 MSG).

Let's not be tiptoeing around issues when we pray. Jesus is with us and even praying on our behalf. "So let's walk right up to him and get what he is so ready to give" (Hebrews 4:16 MSG). We've been given full access to the Father, full access to the Kingdom. Full, never expiring, unrestricted, complete and free access.

Let's start walking in it.

LET US THEN APPROACH GOD'S THRONE OF GRACE WITH CONFIDENCE, SO THAT WE MAY RECEIVE MERCY AND FIND GRACE TO HELP US IN OUR TIME OF NEED.

HEBREWS 4:16

Father, I come to Your throne with confidence, ready to receive Your offer of help. Thank You that Your mercy has removed all barriers between us and enables me to draw near. I will walk boldly in Your authority knowing I have full access to the resources of Heaven.

Stop Your Flapping

AIMÉE

I watch from my window as the birds fly past me, spellbound by their graceful soaring. A pattern emerges as I observe them: There is a momentary flapping of their wings after which they effortlessly glide through the air for significant periods of time, harnessing the power of the wind. Then they repeat this process, each sequence of this pattern propelling them higher and further than before.

'Effortlessly gliding' are not the words that I would have used in the past to describe my own life. I was more prone to frantically flap about, exhausting myself in an effort to gain the smallest momentum or even just keep up with what was already on my plate.

But God used these birds to teach me an important lesson about what it looks like to partner with Him. Yes, there will be times of exertion–of flapping our wings to start or keep momentum going—but the majority of our work is meant to be done by harnessing God's power and riding on the 'wind' of His Spirit.

In Zechariah 4, God spoke these now infamous words to encourage Zerubbabel as he rebuilt the Temple: "This is the word of the Lord to Zerubbabel: 'Not by might nor by power, but by my Spirit,' says the Lord Almighty" (v.6).

Zerubbabel faced a long and difficult task, and God wanted him to know that he wasn't alone in it. He wanted him to understand that the outcome did not rest chiefly in his abilities but in God's. To cement this truth in Israel's thinking, God gave Zechariah a vision of a lampstand that was supernaturally supplied with oil, assuring them of the continued and unlimited supply of God's Spirit for their work. He further promised Zerubbabel that the work he started, *God* would enable him to complete.

Unlike us, God never wearies or tires or runs out; and in everything we undertake, in every season we walk through, He wants to relieve us of carrying the burden alone. His invitation to us is to connect our lives to His unlimited power and resources so that there can be an ease and a grace to our labours. For when we cease our fruitless flapping and instead rely on Him, we are released to soar.

EVEN YOUTHS GROW TIRED AND WEARY, AND YOUNG MEN STUMBLE AND FALL; BUT THOSE WHO HOPE IN THE LORD WILL RENEW THEIR STRENGTH. THEY WILL SOAR ON WINGS LIKE EAGLES; THEY WILL RUN AND NOT GROW WEARY, THEY WILL WALK AND NOT BE FAINT.

ISAIAH 40:30-31

Father, I may tire and grow weary, but You do not. You are my source and my strength, so I place my hope in You and I arise in the power of Your Spirit to do the work before me.

Get Hot and Get Moving

EMILY

Growing up, I had a lava lamp in my room: a silver rocket with lime green wax in bright blue liquid. I loved sitting and watching the wax move, making beautiful shapes and impacting the environment it found itself in.

For lava lamps to work, the wax needs to keep returning to the light. It needs to get hot. A lava lamp doesn't work if the wax isn't heated up. The Church doesn't work if it isn't heated up either. Jesus rebuked the lukewarm church in Laodicea for exactly this reason: "I know your works: you are neither cold nor hot. Would that you were either cold or hot!" (Revelation 3:15 ESV).

Revelation 3 goes on to say that though we may think we're rich, prospering, and don't need anything, all the while we're actually "wretched, pitiable, poor, blind, and naked" (v.17).

It would be foolish for the wax to think that it can climb to the height of the lava lamp in its own strength. It's only because of its proximity to the light that it can be transformed and make beautiful shapes in its surroundings. The further away from the light it travels, the colder and less effective it becomes, and the quicker it sinks.

When the wax is close to the light, it can absorb the light's energy and fulfil its purpose in its environment. It needs to continually return to the light to remain effective and have impact. Let's not mistakenly think we can start off with the Light of life and then climb through life in our own strength. We need to continually return to Jesus, continually allow Him to heat us up where we have grown cold, so that we can continue to make beautiful shapes in the particular environment He's placed us in.

If you want to let your light shine in your home, workplace, and relationships, then you need to return to *the* Light and let Him make you hot. Sometimes the process of heating up can be intense: "Those whom I love, I reprove and discipline" (v.19), but I promise you it's worth it.

No one wants to be a cold, hard lump of wax in the world. Come to the Light—get hot and get moving!

I CORRECT AND DISCIPLINE EVERYONE I LOVE. SO BE DILIGENT AND TURN FROM YOUR INDIFFERENCE.

REVELATION 3:19 NLT

Father, I don't want to be cold or indifferent. I receive Your correction and move close to the warmth of Your light, allowing it to revive my heart that I might share Your beauty wherever I go.

Bring Your Questions

AIMÉE

"But why Mummy?" My then two-year-old was bombarding me with a barrage of questions as we drove home. And despite my best efforts, my answers didn't appear to satisfy him–because the 'but whys?' kept coming for what seemed like an eternity! *What is it about being in a car that seems to invite an onslaught of questions from our kids?*

Children aren't the only ones who have questions. As we get older, though, we tend to stop asking them—and we especially stop asking them of God. Yet just because we don't give a voice to our questions doesn't mean they're not there. Unspoken, they swirl around in the depths of our hearts sowing seeds of doubt and discontent.

Why didn't You heal her?
When will it be my turn?
What am I meant to do?
Where are You in this God?
How come my prayers never seem to get answered?

I've learned, however, that God doesn't have a problem with all my questions. In fact, He welcomes them; He invites me, even, to bring them *to* Him and wrestle them through *with* Him.

David knew this truth. That's why the Psalms are full of his questions and his complaints. He understood that they were better brought into the light of God's presence than left to murmur in the dark. In Psalm 62:8 he tells us: "Trust in Him at all times, O people; pour out your hearts to Him, for God is our refuge" (NIV).

God is meant to be our refuge; the safe place where we can pour out our hearts and our questions. David would go on to say in verse 11 that God is loving and strong. God is strong enough to take our heaviest questions; and while we may not always discover the answers that we were looking for, as we pour out our hearts, leaning into His strength and the depths of His love, we encounter the ultimate answer: We encounter *Him*.

Hold nothing back from God. Trust Him at all times and with all things, and allow Him to become the only answer you need.

I WAIT QUIETLY BEFORE GOD, FOR MY VICTORY COMES FROM HIM. HE ALONE IS MY ROCK AND MY SALVATION, MY FORTRESS WHERE I WILL NEVER BE SHAKEN.

PSALM 62:1–2 NLT

Father, I know that You are loving and strong. You are my safe place to question and wrestle. I commit to hold nothing back from You but to pour it all out and trust You with my heart.

Hypnotising Frogs

EMILY

Did you know that it's possible to hypnotise a frog by putting it on its back and gently stroking its belly? Being so relaxed and comfortable allows the frog to become disconnected from the real world and zone out.

Have you ever been hypnotised by your own comfort? I know I have. Lockdown living, while filled with many challenges, afforded me the opportunity to serve, well, me. When it's the law to stay home, to distance yourself from others, and to get comfortable in your own bubble, it's very hard to re-enter reality when that bubble has popped.

Suddenly, serving in. . . doesn't seem so appealing—the setting up, the planning, the work, the hours, those that take you for granted, those that undermine your efforts, those that refuse to roll up their sleeves and show up to share the load. . . Without warning we find ourselves choosing to have a little lie down and stroke our bellies because, well, it feels nice and is way more comfortable.

But that's not faithful living. Peter writes that we each have "received a gift in order to serve others" and that we "should use it faithfully" (1 Peter 4:10 NiRV).

Serving one another is very different from disconnecting from one another. When we're focused on fulfilling our desires and hypnotised by chasing comfort we cease to see things as they really are. We cease to hear the needs of those around us. We cease to connect with people as we approach them more like projects. We cease to use the gifts God has given us to serve. We cease to be faithful. We've zoned out from the calling God has placed on our lives.

As Christians, we are called to be the hands and feet of Jesus, to serve one another in love, to use the gifts, skills, and talents we've been blessed with to go into the world and make a positive impact for Jesus. Friend, we can't do that while reclining and rubbing our bellies. Let's get to work.

EACH OF YOU RECEIVED A SPIRITUAL GIFT. GOD HAS SHOWN YOU HIS GRACE IN GIVING YOU DIFFERENT GIFTS. AND YOU ARE LIKE SERVANTS WHO ARE RESPONSIBLE FOR USING GOD'S GIFTS. SO BE GOOD SERVANTS AND USE YOUR GIFTS TO SERVE EACH OTHER.

I PETER 4:10 ICB

Father, I will not squander the gifts You've given me but will roll up my sleeves and serve diligently. I trust You to establish the works of my hands that I might bless others and bring You glory.

Moved by Compassion

AIMÉE

After a night in town at one of our city's oldest and fanciest theatres, we found ourselves confronted with the plight of the homeless. The contrast was stark. It was the first time my daughters had come face-to-face with a problem they had only previously heard of, and their young hearts were troubled. "Was there anything they could do?" they asked. "Could they buy a meal for the couple sitting begging by the door?"

Stories move me. It's not uncommon when I'm reading or watching something for the tears to well up and my throat to constrict. I willingly and instinctively identify with a character's pain; their story and my own seem to merge as I share in the emotions of their suffering. My children frequently groan and berate me when they see this happening. "It's just a story, Mum," they tell me. Truthfully, I've worried about their inability to sympathise—even lectured them to be more compassionate. But that night, as I saw how soft their hearts were to the suffering they encountered, I was challenged that perhaps it was my own heart that needed inspecting. Sadly, my empathy doesn't always spill over into real life. Overwhelmed by the enormity of people's pain and suffering, my heart can tend to shut down in an effort to self-protect and keep my sense of powerlessness at bay.

The gospels tell us that Jesus was "moved by compassion" (Matthew 9:36 NKJV). He healed the sick, fed the hungry, embraced the outcasts, restored the sinner, and ultimately suffered on the Cross to show us the depths of the Father's compassion.

Our word compassion comes from the Latin, *compati*, meaning 'to suffer with'. It challenges us not to leave people alone in their suffering but to participate in it *with* them; to walk alongside and help them carry their burden of pain; to allow our tears to give way to action.

God doesn't want us to shut down to the pain of this world because it feels too big. Instead, He invites us to share in the story of Scripture—to demonstrate His compassion for our sin and brokenness, one person at a time, just as Jesus did. *Who is God inviting you to walk with today?*

BUT WHEN HE SAW THE MULTITUDES, HE WAS MOVED WITH COMPASSION FOR THEM, BECAUSE THEY WERE WEARY AND SCATTERED, LIKE SHEEP HAVING NO SHEPHERD. THEN HE SAID TO HIS DISCIPLES, "THE HARVEST TRULY IS PLENTIFUL, BUT THE LABOURERS ARE FEW.

MATTHEW 9:36-37 NKJV

Father, thank You that You invite me to continue the works of Jesus. I will not shut off the suffering of this world but allow myself to be moved by compassion. I will walk alongside the lonely, lift up the hands of the weary, and suffer with them that they might experience Your love.

A New Thing

EMILY

Like many children growing up, I had a small blanket as a comforter. Unlike many children, however, instead of cuddling it with my face or hands when I went to bed, I would put it by my feet and twist it between my toes, passing it from one foot to the other.

Fast forward thirty years and I was in bed unwell. I woke up from a nap and realised that, in my sleep, I had taken off my thick, fluffy socks and was playing with them with my feet.

Apart from being mildly bemused by this occurrence, it led me to consider the following: *Why is it that when we're uncomfortable we return to what is familiar?* Take for example when we're ill, we tend to crave the food our mum made us as a kid. It's familiar; it's safe; it reminds us of our childhood when life was more secure and predictable—when we were given what we wanted and our needs were taken care of.

In unknown or wilderness times it can be tempting to go back to what we know—because, well, we know it. It worked in the past and so it'll work again. *Right?* Creatures of habit that we are, the old and familiar comforts us and makes us feel safe. But it can also stop us from moving forward and experiencing the new things God wants to do.

Just as you don't put new wine into old wineskins (Matthew 9:17), sometimes we need to leave our comforters behind and be prepared to grow up into the new without reverting backwards. Don't get me wrong—that's scary. Stepping into the unknown and walking in faith leaves us vulnerable and open. But God doesn't want us to miss what He's doing, so He says to us "See, I am doing a new thing! Now it springs up; do you not perceive it?" (Isaiah 43:19).

God is not predictable, so we need to stop trying to treat Him as if He'll only work in the ways He has in the past. We can't keep returning to the old if we want to experience the new. Be brave this week; step away from the old. Ask God to show you the new things He's doing that will bring direction and life, "a way in the wilderness and streams in the wasteland" (Isaiah 43:19).

"FORGET ABOUT WHAT'S HAPPENED; DON'T KEEP GOING OVER OLD HISTORY. BE ALERT, BE PRESENT. I'M ABOUT TO DO SOMETHING BRAND-NEW."

ISAIAH 43:19 MSG

Father, I refuse to put You in a box of small-mindedness that says You only work one way. I am attentive to Your Word, ready to hear Your instruction for this day. Expectant and excited for all You plan to do in and through my life, I am alert to Your promptings.

Take the Wheel

AIMÉE

I am a terrible passenger—just ask my husband! All my fears and anxieties seem to rise to the surface and my heart starts racing. I've even been known to scream. All this has nothing to do with my husband's driving and everything to do with the fact that I am no longer in control.

In Colossians 2:6-7, Paul writes this: "So then, just as you received Christ Jesus as Lord, continue to live in him, rooted and built up in him, strengthened in the faith as you were taught and overflowing with thankfulness."

A 'lord' is 'he to whom a person or things belong, about which he has the power of deciding. One supreme in authority'. We love to talk about receiving Jesus as our friend, as our healer, as our light and our life, and even as our Saviour—*but as our Lord?* Well, that can be a different story. Perhaps we fear losing our semblance of control or worry that we will somehow be diminished if we allow Him this place of supreme authority. Yet the simple truth is that without receiving Him as Lord, we cannot truly know Him in these other capacities; we cannot enter into the fullness of all that He offers us.

So Paul tells us to be 'rooted' in Christ. In Ephesians he expands on this idea, praying that we would be rooted and established in love, so we would have the power to grasp the magnitude of Christ's love for us and thereby be filled with all the fullness of God (3:17-19). When our roots are planted firmly in the soil of Christ's love we will no longer be afraid of receiving Him as Lord, because His perfect love drives out fear (1 John 4:18).

Do not believe the lie that submitting to Christ as Lord will diminish you. The abundant life Jesus invites us to live through Him *begins* when we receive Him as Lord. His lordship is essential to our growth; essential to the fullness we are promised in Christ. But this 'receiving' is not a one-off event—it is a lifestyle. We must *continue* to receive Him as Lord, day by day, even moment by moment; rooting ourselves in His immeasurable love and allowing Him to take His rightful place—in the driver's seat.

"AND I PRAY THAT YOU, BEING
ROOTED AND ESTABLISHED IN
LOVE, MAY HAVE POWER. . . TO
GRASP HOW WIDE AND LONG AND
HIGH AND DEEP IS THE LOVE OF
CHRIST, AND TO KNOW THIS LOVE
THAT SURPASSES KNOWLEDGE—
THAT YOU MAY BE FILLED TO THE
MEASURE OF ALL THE FULLNESS
OF GOD.'

EPHESIANS 3:17B-19

Father, I receive Christ as Lord today.
I relinquish my need to be in control, and I
allow Him the place of supreme authority in
my life that I might experience the fullness
of all that You have purposed for me.

Treble Clef Scribbles

EMILY

When my daughter was six, she tried teaching herself the piano using an online app. As a child of two piano teachers myself, I was curious to see just how effective this app would be. After a couple of weeks of intermittent practice, I discovered a scrap of paper with a piece of music written on it.

The faint pencil marked the cutest treble clef scribbles, bars, a good attempt at notation, and underneath, some incorrectly spelt lyrics that expressed the heart of my little girl. It was a long way from perfection, but from her limited resources, she used what she had to bring an offering of love.

It reminded me of the story of the widow's mite. Her resources were scarce, but her offering was great: "The rich have plenty; they gave only what they did not need. This woman is very poor. But she gave all she had" (Mark 12:44 ICB).

You don't need to be a virtuoso to worship well. You can even be a six-year-old with limited understanding, because Jesus isn't interested in the size or skill of our offering but the place it comes from.

I've been challenged by my daughter to consider where my worship comes from. Is it an overflow of what's in my heart? Or does it come from a place of habit, or from the surplus time, money, and energy I have, with little thought or intention behind it? How often do we give to God what we 'do not need'? Writing her song would have taken my daughter extensive time, energy, thought, and perseverance. It was a big effort, and it was costly. *Can I say the same of my own offerings?*

Don't let your limitations limit your praise. It doesn't matter where your starting point is, or what your circumstances are, there's a worship and offering opportunity inside every one of us. Looking at my girl's song I was reminded that it doesn't take much to worship. All it takes is willingness and bravery to offer what little we have. So let's not give Jesus our leftovers. He sees your heart, let's give from there.

FOR THEY GAVE A TINY PART OF THEIR SURPLUS, BUT SHE, POOR AS SHE IS, HAS GIVEN EVERYTHING SHE HAD TO LIVE ON.

MARK 12:44 NLT

Father, You are worthy of worship, worthy of all I have to give. So today, I hold nothing back. I bring all that I am as an offering and present it before You—faltering and limited as it may be, it is Yours. You are my everything and I love You.

For When You Stumble

AIMÉE

We were newbie homeschoolers when we decided to give roller-skating a go and join the local social session. My girls had never skated before and were determined to master it. Week by week their confidence grew, and they moved from timidly holding on to the side of the rink to skating on their own in the centre.

But there was one occasion where one of my daughters couldn't get any skates to fit properly and had to try rollerblades instead. It was a completely different sensation, and she found it much harder to balance. She needed my help, and that day, we made our way around the rink hand-in-hand. No matter how often she stumbled, she kept persevering—and every time she fell, I helped her get back up, continually cheering her on.

Afterwards, I was reminded of David's words in Psalm 37:23-24: "The Lord directs the steps of the godly. He delights in every detail of their lives. Though they stumble, they will never fall, for the Lord holds them by the hand" (NLT).

Ponder these words for a moment. David tells us that God delights in every detail of our lives; yet in the same breath, he tells us that when we stumble, God is with us, lifting us back up with His own hands. This means God's delight in us is not dependent upon us getting it all 'right'. He knows we will make mistakes, and He stays close to ensure that those mistakes don't derail us.

I don't know about you, but every day I stumble in some way. Some days it's just little things—I wish I'd been on time, responded with more kindness, or been a little more patient. Other days I stumble in ways that let's just say I'll keep to the pages of my journal! Yet, I find comfort in knowing that God delights in me and is there holding my hand when I falter.

Don't be deterred by how you might have stumbled. Let God take you by the hand and lift you back up. Be like my daughter and keep going, knowing that He is cheering you on!

SO DO NOT FEAR, FOR I AM WITH
YOU; DO NOT BE DISMAYED, FOR I
AM YOUR GOD. I WILL STRENGTHEN
YOU AND HELP YOU; I WILL UPHOLD
YOU WITH MY RIGHTEOUS RIGHT
HAND.

ISAIAH 41:10

Father, I enter today knowing that I am held by You.
I pause to feel Your delight in me and to remember
that even if I should stumble, You will not let me fall.

Chocolate Milk

EMILY

A liquid is immiscible with another liquid when it can't form a homogeneous mixture when added together. It's a bit of a tongue twister so let me break it down. Think about oil and vinegar in a salad. You can shake them together all you like, but they remain immiscible—together, but separate. However, consider chocolate syrup and milk: shake those together and you suddenly have chocolate milk. That's because they're miscible liquids and can form a homogeneous mixture—the components combining to form one uniform thing.

John tells us that we are not to love the world or anything in it, warning us that "If anyone loves the world, love for the Father is not in them" (1 John 2:15). Christians must be immiscible as far as the world is concerned. We are in it, but not of it. We mustn't become homogeneous when things get shaken up! However, we know that we are to love the people of the world—they are God's children, made in His image—and we know that we're to love and care for the planet: So what does it mean to "not love the world"?

We are to ensure that we don't start to love society's united rebellion against God. We mustn't get sucked into our culture's self-promoting, controlling way of living that lulls us into ignoring God. The world wants us to love it. It wants our time, dedication, effort, money, and attention—and we simply can't be giving that to the world and Jesus simultaneously.

It comes down to attraction.

The oil and vinegar can't mix with one another because the molecules aren't attracted enough to each other; the oil loves the oil particles too much to consider becoming one with the vinegar. If we are to remain in the world (as Jesus prayed for us in John 17) but not love it, then we need to make sure that nothing the world offers supersedes Jesus' attraction.

So the next time you're drinking some chocolate milk, ask the Holy Spirit to reveal any areas where you've become a little too homogeneously aligned with the world. Or when you pour a vinaigrette over your salad, pause and consider the last thing Jesus asked you to do. Then go and do it—immiscibly.

I HAVE GIVEN THEM YOUR WORD.
AND THE WORLD HATES THEM
BECAUSE THEY DO NOT BELONG
TO THE WORLD, JUST AS I DO NOT
BELONG TO THE WORLD. I'M NOT
ASKING YOU TO TAKE THEM OUT
OF THE WORLD, BUT TO KEEP THEM
SAFE FROM THE EVIL ONE. THEY DO
NOT BELONG TO THIS WORLD ANY
MORE THAN I DO.

JOHN 17:14-16 NLT

Father, You have created me to be in the world but
not of it—I am set apart and holy because You
are holy. I walk in Jesus' authority and align
myself with His ways, being obedient
to all You're calling me to do and be.

Free on the Inside

AIMÉE

It is one of those days that will be forever etched into my memory. I had gone upstairs to call the kids for dinner when I discovered that my then four-year-old had had a silent tantrum and, in mere minutes, destroyed the near picture-perfect room she shared with her sister.

The mess in front of me instantly struck a chord. It felt like a metaphor for my life at that time. Five months earlier, my life had been mostly neat and tidy, and I had felt relatively in control. Circumstances had long since ripped this façade away from me, exposing the shadowy mess that had been lurking in the depths of my heart.

Charles C. Colton once said: "Life isn't like a book. Life isn't logical or sensible or orderly. Life is a mess most of the time. And theology must be lived in the midst of that mess." As I spent the next hour sorting and returning everything to its rightful place, God reminded me that while mess is inevitable, it is not always bad. If we allow it to, it can compel us to clean-up, to get rid of rubbish, and rearrange what we have decided to keep. And as we sort through the mess, we discover truth.

In John 8:32, Jesus said, ". . . you will know the truth, and the truth will set you free." While the journey of unveiling truth is seldom neat, tidy, or predictable, when we find it, it ultimately brings us freedom. I had been fighting against anything that exposed my weaknesses or left me vulnerable, and the result was a curated life on the outside that was not replicated on the inside. God's heart was to move me from the outward appearance of goodness and wholeness to that being my actual internal reality. He wanted to set me free—and He wasn't afraid of using mess to do so.

I threw some pretty epic tantrums myself in that season. Yet as God helped me to clean up the aftermath, I realised my own need for a Saviour—for the One who is *the truth*, whose grace is always enough, who is strong when I am weak, and who loves me completely—even on the days when it is all a mess. And the truth of my need was the doorway to wholeness and freedom.

We may crave order and control, but friend, can I encourage you today to stop fearing the messy complicated places of life. God is waiting to meet you there.

SO IF THE SON SETS YOU FREE, YOU WILL BE FREE INDEED.

JOHN 8:36

Father, I choose today to embrace the mess and do the work of sorting through and cleaning up my inner life. I believe that Your heart is for me to truly be whole and to walk in freedom and I refuse to settle for anything less.

Audacious Faith

EMILY

Did you know that the minute hand on London's Big Ben travels 190 kilometres per year? The small, incremental steps it makes as it creeps round minute by minute add up to a considerable distance. When you look at the clock it might seem that the hand isn't going very far, but in the faithful perseverance of measured timekeeping it soon enough 'clocks up' quite the journey.

We can learn a thing or two about going the distance from Big Ben. *How often do we give up or abandon hope because things don't seem to change?* We feel like the effort to be kind is wasted, the energy it takes to forgive is futile, the prayer is falling on deaf ears...

Eugene H. Peterson wrote in his book "A Long Obedience in the Same Direction: Discipleship in an Instant Society," "Perseverance does not mean 'perfection'. It means that we keep going. We do not quit when we find that we are not yet mature and there is a long journey still before us."

The widow in Luke 18 and the friend in Luke 11 were both persistent. Both had audacious faith and didn't give up. They kept knocking, kept asking, and Jesus held up their perseverance as examples for us all. They are an example of why we must "not get tired of doing what is good. At just the right time we will reap a harvest of blessing if we don't give up" (Galatians 6:9 NLT).

I don't know what it is that is draining you right now. I don't know the situation that makes you want to give up—the uncertainty of future plans, the fraught and fractious relationship, the disappointment and pain of bad news. But I do know this: God doesn't change. He is unfaltering in bringing new mercies each morning. Just as we rely on time to keep a steady pace through life, we can rely on His steadfastness to be with us and equip us with all we need to keep going.

So make the small step today, whisper the desperate prayer, practice patience with the toddler, call the forgotten friend, "be strong and do not give up, for your work will be rewarded" (2 Chronicles 15:7). You *will* go the distance if you are obedient in the seemingly insignificant, knowing that nothing you do for God "is a waste of time or effort" (1 Corinthians 15:58 MSG).

THEREFORE, MY DEAR BROTHERS AND SISTERS, STAND FIRM. LET NOTHING MOVE YOU. ALWAYS GIVE YOURSELVES FULLY TO THE WORK OF THE LORD, BECAUSE YOU KNOW THAT YOUR LABOUR IN THE LORD IS NOT IN VAIN.

I CORINTHIANS 15:58

Father, I will not grow weary in doing what is good but be steadfast in obedience. I will boldly persist in moving forward no matter how small the steps I take seem, knowing my efforts are not in vain; my work reaps a harvest of blessing and brings You glory.

Take a Different Approach

AIMÉE

She had been my 'soul sister'. But now, I felt like a stranger in her presence. She kept me at arms length and I felt the truth of Proverbs 18:19 deeply— "an offended friend is harder to win back than a fortified city. Arguments separate friends like a gate locked with bars" (NLT). I imagine at some time we've all found ourselves here: Standing on the other side of the gate wondering how to break through the barrier of offence back to relationship. Back to connection.

Offences hurt and arguments wound. The Hebrew verb translated as offended is *pōša'*, and it means 'to rebel, to transgress, to revolt; to be rebelled against'. This is often how we feel when we face conflict in our relationships—as though who we are and what we value has been attacked. So we fight back, retaliating in kind, all the while perpetuating the cycle of hurt. The walls get higher, the locks more difficult to crack.

Jesus commands us to take a different approach: "But to you who are listening I say: Love your enemies, do good to those who hate you, bless those who curse you, pray for those who mistreat you... Then your reward will be great, and you will be sons of the Most High, because He is kind to the ungrateful and wicked. Be merciful, just as your Father is merciful" (Luke 6:27 & 35b-36, NIV).

It's counter-intuitive and counter-cultural, but in my own journey, I have found this to be a powerful and effective strategy, one that not only protects my own heart, but also gives me God's heart for the one who has wounded me. You cannot stay bound by offence when you are praying. Healthy boundaries may need to stay in place but walls of bitterness and unforgiveness come crashing down when we are on our knees for those who hurt and oppose us.

We live in a world that defends the right to be offended; to live as a victim. God invites us to instead live as sons and daughters of the Most High, entrusting our hurts and injustices to Him—the One who judges justly (1 Peter 2:23)—and refusing to be ensnared by offence.

Who is God asking you to pray for? Invite Him to empower you to love them as He does.

BE EVEN-TEMPERED, CONTENT WITH SECOND PLACE, QUICK TO FORGIVE AN OFFENSE. FORGIVE AS QUICKLY AND COMPLETELY AS THE MASTER FORGAVE YOU. AND REGARDLESS OF WHAT ELSE YOU PUT ON, WEAR LOVE. IT'S YOUR BASIC, ALL-PURPOSE GARMENT. NEVER BE WITHOUT IT.

COLOSSIANS 3:13-14 MSG

Father, I resolve that I will not be easily offended. I will love my enemies, do good to those who hate me, bless those who curse me, and pray for those who mistreat me—I will wear love at all times.

Sausage Fingers

EMILY

As a child I always wanted to be involved in show business somehow, particularly if it involved a screen. I also happened to hate my fingers as a kid. I always thought they were short and fat, like sausages. So imagine my surprise when it was precisely *because* of my stubby fingers that I was offered the opportunity to be part of the biggest-budget TV series ever. Landing the highly coveted role of 'hand double' led to several other roles and eventually a full-time job on crew.

I'm still blown away that God would use my fingers to answer a deep longing I had since squashed, believing it was too frivolous to entertain; that in His kindness He would go beyond my wildest dreams or what I never conceived possible (Ephesians 3:20) to give me the experience of a lifetime.

But this is how He works.

We so often get distracted by our perceived inadequacies and failings—the aspects of our personality and appearance that can feel 'too much' or 'less than'—that we write ourselves off as 'unusable' by God. But Scripture reassures us He not only uses but *chooses* the foolish, weak, lowly, and despised things to accomplish His purposes (1 Corinthians 1:27). He uses "the things that are not—to nullify the things that are" (1 Corinthians 1:28). The last thing I ever would have thought God could use would be my fingers. Yet He does these things to help us understand just how glorious He is.

The thing that floored me about this whole experience was that working on a TV set isn't exactly akin to curing cancer, solving the climate crisis, or eliminating poverty. But God's not only interested in choosing us to achieve things *for* Him. Sometimes He chooses us in our smallness and grants us the desires of our heart, simply out of His sheer love for us (Deuteronomy 7:7).

What is it that prevents you from believing God could display His glory in your life? What is that deep dream you squashed long ago thinking it was too frivolous to entertain? Dare to dream again that God might just want to use the very thing you despise to shower you with blessing and show you just how much He loves you.

GOD CHOSE THE LOWLY THINGS OF
THIS WORLD AND THE DESPISED
THINGS—AND THE THINGS THAT
ARE NOT—TO NULLIFY THE THINGS
THAT ARE, SO THAT NO ONE MAY
BOAST BEFORE HIM.

I CORINTHIANS 1:28-29

Father, I thank You for choosing me to display
Your glory. I will not despise how You have made
me but bring You every aspect of who I am;
use me to accomplish Your purposes. I expand
my thinking and dare to dream big with You.

Confident in His Constancy

AIMÉE

In the early years of our marriage, I regularly prayed Psalm 112 over my husband. We were in a season where we found ourselves continually hammered by tests and trials, and one verse in particular, where the psalmist declares that the righteous will "have no fear of bad news; their hearts are steadfast, trusting in the Lord," caught my attention (Psalm 112:7). In my youthful naivety (and desperation), I clung to this verse, believing it to be a promise we wouldn't continue to get bad news. Experience subsequently taught me it was describing the posture the righteous were to take *when* they get bad news.

Bad news comes to us all, but as God's children, we don't need to be gripped by fear when it does. We can be steadfast and secure because our trust is not in changing circumstances, but in an unchanging, unshakeable God who sees the beginning from the end and weaves all the in-between for our good and His glory. It is His constancy that gives us confidence we will one day "look in triumph on [our] foes" (v.8).

But it's not all a distant future hope. The psalmist also tells us, "Even in darkness light dawns for the upright, for those who are gracious, compassionate, and righteous. Good will come to those who are generous and lend freely, who conduct their affairs with justice." (vv.4-5).

No matter how dark life seems, God's light is always present; it rises upon us and through us. We allow His light to illuminate the darkness we all face as we give expression to the heart of God—as we show grace and compassion, walk according to His ways, sow generously, and value justice. These acts demonstrate our trust that He is Lord over all—and it's this truth that enables our hearts to remain steady when everything around us is shaking.

Look for His light today and keep trusting in Him, knowing that "blessed are those who fear the Lord" (v.1).

SURELY THE RIGHTEOUS WILL NEVER BE SHAKEN; THEY WILL BE REMEMBERED FOREVER. THEY WILL HAVE NO FEAR OF BAD NEWS; THEIR HEARTS ARE STEADFAST, TRUSTING IN THE LORD. THEIR HEARTS ARE SECURE, THEY WILL HAVE NO FEAR; IN THE END THEY WILL LOOK IN TRIUMPH ON THEIR FOES.

PSALM 112:6-8

Father, You are my constant. You make me steadfast—even in my darkest moments Your light shines bright. The way I live reflects my trust in Your goodness; I believe that You will enable me to triumph over my enemies.

He Must Increase

EMILY

This week, my kids and I conducted a very important experiment: Can you tell the difference between corn, wheat, oat, and rice Cheerios with your eyes closed? It was the ultimate taste test. Could they identify what was underneath the sugary exterior even though the outside coating was identical? It turns out they could.

It made me wonder: *Can other people tell the difference between those of us who call ourselves Christians and those who don't?* For the most part we all have the same outside coating. We have nice clothes, great schools, and pretty decent homes. We all talk about and seek to live lives that are authentic, kind and considerate. *So, if the exterior is the same, what makes the difference underneath?*

Throughout the book of John, Jesus says there are things that will set us apart and show the world that we're His disciples. The world will know we belong to Him when we hold to His teaching (8:31), when we're fruitful (15:8), and when we love one another (John 13:35).

These things are all interconnected. If we hold to His teaching then we will be fruitful and we will love one another. It sounds fairly simple when you say it like that. But the reality of living this way is much tougher—loving and praying for your enemy, turning the other cheek when someone has wronged you, loving and serving those that drive you nuts, loving and caring for the last, the least, and the lost. . . Some days I find it hard enough loving the people I've chosen to love let alone the weird, wacky, and downright peculiar.

The outside may look similar, but we're not the same on the inside. As John reminds us, "Dear children. . . the one who is in you is greater than the one who is in the world" (1 John 4:4). God dwells within us! He has equipped us with every spiritual blessing so we might complete every good work. He supplies us with every good thing needed to fulfil His purposes. He has placed His Spirit within us.

Don't despair if you think you're not making the impact you want to as a disciple. Go back to His teaching and, like Paul, ask Jesus to increase as we decrease (John 3:30). You can only do it with His help (Hebrews 13:21 NiRV).

BUT YOU BELONG TO GOD, MY DEAR
CHILDREN. YOU HAVE ALREADY
WON A VICTORY OVER THOSE
PEOPLE, BECAUSE THE SPIRIT WHO
LIVES IN YOU IS GREATER THAN THE
SPIRIT WHO LIVES IN THE WORLD.

I JOHN 4:4 NLT

Father, thank You that Your Spirit within me
is greater than the one that is in the world.
He supplies me with everything I need
to walk in obedience, hold fast to Your
teaching, and grow in love. I willingly
decrease that You might increase in my life.

It's a Heart Thing

AIMÉE

"Because I said so."

They were words that my mother said to me. Words that I now find myself saying to my own children when my first explanation doesn't suffice and they continue to question my instructions.

If I'm being honest, I cringe a little when these words come out of my mouth. I might even go so far as to say I hate that I resort to using them. Because here's the thing: I don't want to demand obedience. I want my kids to *want* to be obedient. I want them to trust that I have their best at heart; to believe that if I ask something of them it is because of my love for them.

In John 15:9, Jesus invites us to abide in His love for us, to live a life that is anchored and held by that love. He then goes on to say: "When you obey my commandments, you remain in my love, just as I obey my Father's commandments and remain in his love" (v. 10 NLT).

The word used for obey, was the Greek word *tēreō* which meant 'to attend to carefully; to take care of; to guard'. Obedience is an action that stems from an internal position. It is not about earning love, but responding to it—it's a heart connection. When we love someone, we care about the things that matter to them. Because Jesus loved the Father, He lived a life of surrendered obedience, carefully attending to the things that the Father asked Him to. And now, He invites us to do the same.

When we choose the path of obedience, it keeps us continually connected not only to the truth that we are loved but to the experience of being loved. And the fruit of our choice to be obedient is that our joy will be complete (John 15:11). It will abound and overflow.

What is Jesus asking you to be faithful to attend to this week? Let the depths of His love assure you that you can trust Him with the task before you.

WHOEVER HAS MY COMMANDS AND KEEPS THEM IS THE ONE WHO LOVES ME. THE ONE WHO LOVES ME WILL BE LOVED BY MY FATHER, AND I TOO WILL LOVE THEM AND SHOW MYSELF TO THEM.

JOHN 14:21

Father, I love You. I want to protect our heart-connection and to be faithful with the things You entrust to me. I choose to live a life of surrendered obedience, and I thank You, Holy Spirit, that You will empower me to be a trustworthy servant.

Beyond Survival

EMILY

"I don't want to survive; I want to live!"

The captain in the movie "Wall-E" has had enough of floating around, living a mundane existence focused on simply surviving in space. For centuries they've stayed aboard the aptly named ship "Axiom" without questioning their situation, but when life is discovered on the supposedly doomed planet earth, it stirs something within the captain to recognise that merely existing isn't living.

Surviving is not thriving.

I wonder if there are areas in our lives where we're surviving because we've settled on the idea that it's just the way it is. There's no hope for change, and our society, family, health, or any number of life categories are established and unchangeable. They're axioms. Things are the way they are, so you had better just get on and survive.

Jesus has other ideas. He came to give us life and life to the full (John 10:10); He's all about His kids thriving and not just surviving. The psalmist writes, "You make known to me the path of life; you will fill me with joy in your presence, with eternal pleasures at your right hand" (Psalm 16:11).

Jesus' heart is for us to truly live—experiencing the pleasures of living, existing, working, serving, and loving in His presence. He longs for us to know clarity and direction in the choices we make, and to realise joy and fulfilment as we live in communion with Him. Jesus wants us to rise against the humdrum mundanity, to stop simply existing—and start living.

Where have you found yourself thinking, that's just the way it is? Have you begun to simply survive in areas of your life rather than know the thrilling adventure of thriving when you live hand in hand with Jesus?

There is power in the presence and name of Jesus. He sets us free from a mediocre life and calls us instead to truly start living. Ask Him to set you free again so that you might live fully alive, "animated and motivated by God's Spirit" (Galatians 5:16 MSG).

IT IS FOR FREEDOM THAT CHRIST HAS SET US FREE. . . YOU, MY BROTHERS AND SISTERS, WERE CALLED TO BE FREE.

GALATIANS 5:IA, I3A

Father, I want to do more than just survive; I want life in all its abundance. Holy Spirit make known to me Your paths of life, filling me with the joy of your presence. May Your fruit manifest in my life and enable me to walk in love, joy, peace, patience, kindness, goodness, gentleness, faithfulness, and self-control. I'm fully alive with you.

Beauty in Hard Places

AIMÉE

I'm somewhat of a winter girl. Warm fires, good books, cosy throws, and slow-cooked comfort food at the end of a long day sound like my idea of perfection. As far as spiritual seasons go, winter used to be something I preferred to avoid. However, I've come to realise that God does some of His most beautiful work in the winter seasons.

It was a number of years ago now, in the midst of a dark winter of my own soul, that God revealed this truth to me: The seeds of new life don't begin in the spring but in the winter. It is in the winter that lambs are birthed, barren trees begin to bud, and dormant bulbs begin to push their way up and out of the dark heavy earth that has been concealing their existence. In the midst of the cold and sometimes barren landscape, things of great beauty are being realised.

Yes, 'new things' often spring forth from the most unlikely of places (Isaiah 43:19). But the question that God asked through the prophet Isaiah is so often the question we must ask ourselves: *Will we have eyes to perceive what God is doing? Will we have faith to believe that God is able to bring beauty from our barrenness?*

There can be a fragility to new beginnings. Like lambs born into a harsh climate, we can find ourselves vulnerable; the elements often oppose the new life that is emerging, and we must guard our hope and protect what God is doing within us. We must also make peace with discomfort.

Allowing God to do a fresh new work can feel exposing and confronting, and as with all birthing processes, there is effort involved. But if we are willing to brave the elements, there is also an opportunity for us to draw near and experience God in a deeper way. For just as winter invites us to seek out warmth, the winter seasons of the soul beckon us to draw closer to our Comforter, trusting in His goodness and love for us, and believing in His redemptive ability to bring forth new life.

The winter months can feel relentless, but they are not hopeless. Let's position ourselves for growth and rest in the knowledge that beneath the surface, beauty is waiting to be revealed.

YOU ARE GOOD, AND WHAT YOU
DO IS GOOD; TEACH ME YOUR
DECREES.

PSALM 119:68

Father, I believe that You are able to bring
beauty out of hard places. I open my eyes to see
what You are doing and position myself in faith
for new growth. I will protect what You are
outworking in my life confident that You
are good and will always be good to me.

Bringing Out the God-Colours

EMILY

Every Autumn my attention is captured as I watch the deciduous trees in my neighbourhood undergo transformation.

The process itself is beautiful—but slow. Day to day you can't spot much difference, but over an extended period of time, sure enough, you begin to see the outworking of an internal change. As each leaf gradually shifts and changes colour, the overall effect is powerful and stunning.

Sometimes I think we want personal transformation to happen immediately. We want to go from A to Z without the journey in the middle. We want the resolution, pay cheque, or amazing relationship, without the work to get there. But, if we rushed the transformation process, we'd miss so much colour and beauty. We would have so much less impact if we sought to change in our own rushed timing.

The transformation process happens most fully where the leaves are most exposed to the sunlight. The leaves that were hidden, languishing in the dark, tend to miss out on displaying the full-range of autumnal colours available. They simply wither away to nothing, starved of the light. In the same way, the process of transformation in our own lives is most effective when we position ourselves to have exposure to *the* Light—the Son. And, just like the leaves on the tree were especially stunning when viewed altogether, we will make more of an impact if we do our journey of transformation with others. We each bring our own unique colouring that makes the tree—the body of Christ—majestic in its standing and, together, we can more effectively bring "out the God colours in the world" (Matthew 5:14 MSG).

Don't rush God's perfect timing for the season that you're in. Don't get disheartened if the transformation doesn't happen overnight. You might be providing hope and joy for someone else as they observe your journey or God might be doing vital growth internally that can't be seen immediately on the outside. The leaves aren't stressing about the change, they're letting the sun do its work. We need to let the Son and the Spirit do theirs.

AND WE ALL, WHO WITH UNVEILED FACES CONTEMPLATE THE LORD'S GLORY, ARE BEING TRANSFORMED INTO HIS IMAGE WITH EVER-INCREASING GLORY, WHICH COMES FROM THE LORD, WHO IS THE SPIRIT.

2 CORINTHIANS 3:18

Father, I position myself in Your light that I might become brighter and more vibrant for You. I submit to Your Spirit allowing Him to bring about change in Your perfect timing. I am not rushed or anxious, my heart is in Your safe hands.

Choosing Handkerchiefs

AIMÉE

It's one of those unusual childhood memories that has stayed with me. Perhaps because it was my first encounter with death. The treasures that my great-grandfather—who was quite the collector and bargain hunter—had accumulated were laid out on his lounge floor, and I had been invited to choose something to remember him by. I selected a box of floral handkerchiefs with scalloped edging as my 'inheritance'.

In 1 Samuel 10, Saul is being anointed as king over Israel, and as Samuel pours the oil over his head, he declares that the Lord has anointed him leader over His inheritance. God was entrusting Saul not so much with a geographic region as with the people that He loved. They were who He viewed as His inheritance.

And now, we have this same privilege.

In Ephesians 1:11, Paul writes this: "Through our union with Christ we too have been claimed by God as His own inheritance. Before we were even born, He gave us our destiny; that we would fulfil the plan of God who always accomplishes every purpose and plan in His heart" (TPT).

Think about that for a moment. God, the One to whom the earth and everything in it belongs—who could take His pick from all of the world's riches and treasures—chooses us, claims us as His inheritance.

An inheritance is something that you look after; something that you cultivate and protect and seek to increase. We are immensely valuable to God, and because of this, we can trust that our lives have purpose, and that He will faithfully work with us to fulfil and accomplish those purposes.

What might your life look like if you embraced this truth that you are God's inheritance? If you believed that such is your value and worth, He would choose you above all other treasures?

Today, allow the truth that you not only have an inheritance but that you are *His* inheritance, to permeate all that you think and do.

I PRAY THAT YOUR HEARTS WILL
BE FLOODED WITH LIGHT SO
THAT YOU CAN UNDERSTAND THE
CONFIDENT HOPE HE HAS GIVEN
TO THOSE HE CALLED—HIS HOLY
PEOPLE WHO ARE HIS RICH AND
GLORIOUS INHERITANCE.

EPHESIANS 1:18 NLT

Father, I am humbled and honoured to be Your chosen inheritance. I recognise the value of my life in Your eyes, and I commit to partner with You to see Your plans and purposes realised.

Put on Your Armour

EMILY

I once got burnt. Badly burnt.

You see, I *thought* I had sunblock on. I *thought* I was protected by a shield of lotion—that I hadn't actually put on—then was exposed to the extremely harsh sun for almost two hours in the middle of the day.

At times, it's easy to be deceived into thinking we're protected from external attacks when, in fact, we've left ourselves wide open to getting hurt. I had sunblock; I had exactly what I needed on hand, but left in the bottle it wasn't much use. It needed to be applied and put on to be fully effective.

When Paul writes to the Ephesians, he is clear we're in the midst of a spiritual battle and must put on our armour. We can't assume we are safe or protected when the devil's schemes are involved. Interestingly though, before we put on the armour provided to us, we are commanded to "be strong in the Lord and in His mighty power" (Ephesians 6:10).

Jesus offers us all the strength we need to be fully protected from the intense and fiery attacks the devil will inevitably send our way. It's *Jesus'* strength that is our protection, so we know it is sufficient. To stand firm in His strength we have to first acknowledge Jesus' role, then put on the additional protection we've been given. Much like a sun lotion barrier, "the shield of faith" is the piece of armour that will extinguish the flaming arrows of the enemy.

How readily do we pick up our shield of faith when we get out of bed in the morning to face the day? How often do we leave ourselves exposed to getting burnt simply because we've left Jesus behind when we step out the door?

Each time I go outside, I don't panic about being in the sun, because I know that protection is readily available. In the same way, Jesus has already "disarmed the powers and authorities. . . triumphing over them by the cross" (Colossians 2:15). We may be in the middle of spiritual warfare, but the battle has already been won and the shield we stand behind is the victory of the cross. In the meantime, though, don't forget to put your armour on so you don't get burnt.

AND HAVING DISARMED THE POWERS AND AUTHORITIES, HE MADE A PUBLIC SPECTACLE OF THEM, TRIUMPHING OVER THEM BY THE CROSS.

COLOSSIANS 2:15

Father, I stand firm choosing to put on the spiritual armour You have provided for me. Thank You that I live triumphant in Jesus' victory over sin, the devil, and death.

Magnificent

AIMÉE

For a number of years, we lived on a little peninsula overlooking the ocean. From the early morning light to the way the midday rays seemed to dance upon the waves to the sun-kissed skies at the close of the day, God's creation continually testified to me of His glory and His creativity.

But it wasn't just the ocean that captivated me, it was the night skies too. With no city lights to compete with, the stars shone bright against the velvety darkness and even the planets with their piercing glow were regularly visible.

As I observed the magnificence of these far-away bodies and the vastness and enormity of our galaxy, I was reminded of the bigness of our God.

Colossians 1:16-17 tells us this: "For by him all things were created: things in heaven and on earth, visible and invisible... all things were created by him and for him. He is before all things and in Him all things hold together."

My God created the vast oceans that I looked out upon. My God spoke the stars into being and fashioned the planets in all their mysterious glory. He organised our solar system and mapped out every galaxy. And now, He holds all these things together.

And if He can hold all these things together, He can most certainly hold me.

It can be easy to allow the wonder of who God is to be eclipsed by the magnitude of our problems or by the daily grind. Sometimes we just need to stop—to look up and look around. To survey His creation and remind ourselves of what our God is capable of. As the prophet Jeremiah rightly exclaimed, "Sovereign Lord, you have made the heavens and the earth by your great power and outstretched arm. Nothing is too hard for you" (Jeremiah 32:17).

Be encouraged today that God's got you. His hand is on your life in all its creative power, and there's nothing you are facing that is beyond His abilities.

THE HEAVENS DECLARE THE GLORY OF GOD; THE SKIES PROCLAIM THE WORK OF HIS HANDS. DAY AFTER DAY THEY POUR FORTH SPEECH; NIGHT AFTER NIGHT THEY REVEAL KNOWLEDGE.

PSALM 19:1-2

Father, I worship You. You created the heavens and the earth, and to this day You hold it all together. I believe that You hold me too. I find rest in the truth that nothing is too hard for You.

Firm Foundation

EMILY

One minute you're walking on solid ground, and the next a giant hole in the earth opens up and swallows everything.

Sinkholes: unpredictable, unfair, unexpected, unpleasant, and uninvited. Sinkholes reveal what's going on below the surface. Externally, everything may appear solid and secure but underneath, acidic water, drought, or heavy rain can cause the bedrock to slowly erode and waste away, leaving everything built on top susceptible to come crashing down at any moment.

In 2021, when our city returned to lockdown without warning, it felt a little like a sinkhole had swallowed us up. We thought everything was fine. Life was back to 'normal' and there were no restrictions. Suddenly the ground opened and we found ourselves at the bottom of a 'stay at home', 'work from home', 'school from home' hole, and to be honest, it freaked me out.

Sinkholes can look different for everyone. Perhaps your finances unexpectedly took a hit or a loved one is no longer with you, leaving a gaping hole. Maybe you've been walking and leaning on your intelligence, health, popularity, or freedom for security, and in one moment it's gone. Life as you knew it has been swallowed up and you're left in a hole.

But don't fear. God says, "When the earth goes topsy-turvy and nobody knows which end is up, I nail it all down, I put everything in place again" (Psalm 75:3 MSG). You might be in the bottom of a gaping hole right now wondering how you ended up there. May I remind you that "when the storms of life come" those in Christ "have a lasting foundation" (Proverbs 10:25 NLT).

Jesus is the One who can place us on a firm foundation despite the unpredictability of life. He is the One who "will restore, support, and strengthen you" (1 Peter 5:10 NLT). He is the One to call out to in this topsy-turvy world. Don't let the shifts and changes in the bedrock beneath you be the thing that wipes you out and lands you at the bottom of a hole. Hold fast to Jesus because "he who promised is faithful" (Hebrews 10:23 ESV). He is the only foundation that will never erode or waste away.

WHEN THE TEMPEST PASSES,
THE WICKED IS NO MORE, BUT
THE RIGHTEOUS IS ESTABLISHED
FOREVER.

PROVERBS 10:25 ESV

Father, I will not fear the storms of life. I hold fast to my sure foundation, Jesus, knowing He cannot be moved. He keeps His promises and is faithful to strengthen and sustain me.

Don't Lose Heart

AIMÉE

I was twenty-four years old and a new mum when I found myself navigating some circumstances that were overwhelming, to say the least. I'd headed off to a day retreat hoping to find some encouragement—which I did, albeit not in the form I had anticipated. That day, it was prophesied over me that I was entering a refining and polishing season. *Entering?* I thought I was already there!

Strange as it may sound, this prophesy of hardship was encouraging—the acknowledgement of the nature of the season I was in, coupled with the exhortation to remember the goodness of God and the fruit that would flow from His refining, strengthened me and was part of what enabled me to stay the course at that time. Likewise, Paul and Barnabas encouraged the disciples at Antioch who were suffering to remain true to the faith with these words: "We must go through many hardships to enter the kingdom of God" (Acts 14:22).

Their encouragement did not come in the form of platitudes or great one-liners that white-washed or minimised the persecution they faced. No, like the word I received that day, they proclaimed the reality of suffering, reminding them that the Kingdom of God was their goal and their reward.

If we expect that we will not face adversity—that our faith somehow makes us exempt from the hard stuff—we will soon find ourselves disillusioned with God. Yet equally, expecting to suffer need not condemn us to a life of pessimistic doom and gloom. When we fix our eyes not on what is seen but on that which is unseen and eternal, hope is renewed and becomes our anchor—the hope of who God is and what He is doing in and through us and the knowledge that His Kingdom is unshakeable.

If you find yourself in a season of suffering, don't lose heart, you are not alone and you are not forsaken. You are destined for His Kingdom—may you see it breaking into your life and circumstances even today.

THEREFORE WE DO NOT LOSE HEART. THOUGH OUTWARDLY WE ARE WASTING AWAY, YET INWARDLY WE ARE BEING RENEWED DAY BY DAY. FOR OUR LIGHT AND MOMENTARY TROUBLES ARE ACHIEVING FOR US AN ETERNAL GLORY THAT FAR OUTWEIGHS THEM ALL.

2 CORINTHIANS 4:16-17

Father, I fix my eyes on that which is unseen today and refuse to lose heart. I believe that day by day You are renewing me to receive an eternal glory. Your Kingdom is my goal and my reward.

Hide in Jesus

EMILY

Did you know that snails can sleep for up to three years at a time if the weather doesn't suit them? Snails need moisture to survive, so if the weather is too dry, they need to hunker down and wait for a wetter day.

I feel like a snail sometimes. The climate around me can be arid and dry and, quite frankly, that doesn't always suit me. Perhaps the kids are complaining. Maybe the finances aren't quite stretching to payday. Sometimes relationships are fraught and fractious, and even God seems far away and just out of reach. When life is forecasting a drought, I can be tempted to hide away in my shell where no one can reach me—hidden until the weather shifts and I can emerge as if nothing has happened.

And yet, that's not real life. Unlike snails, we can't just hibernate for three years until circumstances suit us better. Life keeps going and we can't check out until things start looking up.

The Israelites knew something about living day to day in the dry and parched places. The places where, despite God's presence with them, they felt far from Him—unseen and uncared for. For forty years they had to remain in the hot, dry wilderness. No hiding away until the climate changed for *them*. But God was with them, and He provided the exact type of precipitation they needed: bread from heaven.

The Israelites needed to "gather a day's portion every day" (Exodus 16:4), because when you're living in the wilderness, the way to survive is to gather provisions daily. We are not snails. We can't sign off for years at a time. We keep going—day by day. And so we pray, "give us today our daily bread" (Matthew 6:11) knowing that, like the Israelites, we need daily, life-giving sustenance.

When the weather of life isn't to our liking, what we need is the Bread from heaven who "gives life to the world" (John 6:33). Jesus told us that He is the Bread of life and that whoever comes to Him will never hunger or thirst again.

The next time the weather doesn't suit, don't hide away. Hide in Jesus—the only Source of life we ever need.

JESUS SAID, "I AM THE BREAD OF LIFE. THE PERSON WHO ALIGNS WITH ME HUNGERS NO MORE AND THIRSTS NO MORE, EVER."

JOHN 6:35 MSG

Father, no matter the conditions I may face, I choose to hide in Jesus knowing He will provide all that I need. Daily I remind myself to seek my sustenance from You and You alone. You give me life.

Plant Good Seeds

AIMÉE

Once upon a time, I had a vegetable garden. And though this foray into growing our own produce was short-lived, that summer we enjoyed eating what we had grown. We enjoyed our harvest. What I didn't enjoy so much was all the watering and weeding and waiting that preceded it.

As Paul closes his letter to the Galatians, he gives them this often-quoted encouragement: "And don't allow yourselves to be weary or disheartened in planting good seeds, for the season of reaping the wonderful harvest you've planted is coming!" (6:9 TPT).

Weary. I'm sure we've all arrived at that place before. *Maybe you're there now?* Too tired to keep going, the promise of a harvest feels too distant or too removed from today to spur you on.

I've discovered that our hearts need to be set not so much on the timing or even the quantity of the harvest but on the quality of it. We need to love the seeds themselves because of what they represent—to recognise that each seed we sow is in and of itself intrinsically valuable and 'good'.

Robert Louis Stevenson once said, "Don't judge each day by the harvest you reap but by the seeds that you plant." Every day, we have the opportunity to plant Kingdom seeds in our relationships, in our homes and workplaces, and in our communities and nations. Seeds of hope and healing; seeds of truth and transformation; seeds of love and reconciliation. Seeds that release the fruits of the Spirit.

At the time, our seeds may feel insignificant, but even a single seed can be a powerful thing. It has the capacity to reproduce far beyond its size and to keep growing and multiplying even beyond its own lifetime.

Where and how is God inviting you to partner with Him in sowing good seeds today? Be encouraged and strengthened not only by the hope of the harvest but also by the beauty and significance of what you are planting.

LET US NOT BECOME WEARY IN
DOING GOOD, FOR AT THE PROPER
TIME WE WILL REAP A HARVEST IF
WE DO NOT GIVE UP. THEREFORE,
AS WE HAVE OPPORTUNITY, LET US
DO GOOD TO ALL PEOPLE.

GALATIANS 6:9-10A

Father, I believe today is a good day to plant Kingdom seeds. I will be faithful to sow what You have placed in my hand, confident that it carries value, and expectant for the harvest it will yield.

Pay Close Attention

EMILY

What have you looked at today and not seen?

One example I can think of is your nose. Your nose is always visible to you but your mind ignores it through a process called "unconscious selective attention." Our brains constantly make choices to prioritise certain information coming in at the cost of neglecting other information. God has always known this is the case. In Isaiah 42 we read, "You have seen many things, but you pay no attention. . . " (v.20).

There are many scientific experiments investigating why our brains choose to see some things and ignore others, which show that our unconsciously selective brains screen the incoming information based on our goals and emotions. It turns out that what matters to you most, what gets your heart racing, will be the thing you see.

The power of our unconscious is greatest when our attention is under substantial stress. Where we split our attention in our multitasking world of computers versus children, facebook versus family, mobiles versus mates, we are giving more and more responsibility to our unconscious to choose what we see as important. And our unconscious will veer towards that which matters the most.

So, what are you prioritising in your life? What are you giving your attention to?

Jesus tells us to "give your entire attention to what God is doing right now" (Matthew 6:34 MSG). If you don't go 'all in' with your awareness and attention for what God is doing then you may well miss it, or miss Him, altogether.

Just like we can go about our day oblivious to our noses, let's not "become so well-adjusted to [our] culture that [we] fit into it without even thinking." Instead, Paul reminds us that we actively need to "fix our attention on God" (Romans 12:2 MSG). So let's dial down the distractions in order that we might intentionally focus on the One that matters most: The One that will give us the peace we desperately desire; the One who keeps us in the world but not of it (John 17:13-19); the One we're called to fix our eyes on above all else—Jesus.

YOU HAVE SEEN MANY THINGS,
BUT YOU PAY NO ATTENTION; YOUR
EARS ARE OPEN, BUT YOU DO NOT
LISTEN. . . WHICH OF YOU WILL
LISTEN TO THIS OR PAY CLOSE
ATTENTION IN TIME TO COME?

ISAIAH 42:20,23

Father, I fix my attention on You today. I resolve
to not be distracted but to make You my focus,
listening intently to what You are saying and doing.
Jesus, You are my priority and the One that I live for.

My Water-Walking Jesus

AIMÉE

The bay was not calm that day. Much like the night that Peter endeavoured to walk across the lake to Jesus, the wind was blowing strong, and choppy waves stretched out as far as I could see. Facing storms of my own, I envisaged Jesus walking across the water to meet me as I walked along the shore. The Jesus I saw was not perturbed or hindered by the power of the elements. He simply kept walking towards me, their might subdued under His feet.

Ephesians 1 reminds us that God's power is "incomparably great" (v.19). So great that it raised Christ from the dead, and "seated him at [the Father's] right hand in the heavenly realms, far above all rule and authority, power and dominion, and every title that can be given, not only in the present age but also in the one to come" (vv.20-21). And once He was seated, "God placed *all* things under his feet..." (v.22).

That night, as Jesus came towards the disciples, making His way across the stormy lake, He was reminding them that the very thing that they feared—the raging sea—was but a vehicle for Him to come to them. As He conquered what they were most afraid of at that point in time, He was giving them a visual picture: This is not too hard for me.

Jesus walks across the stormy waters of our hearts and circumstances with calm authority, always moving towards us. But more than that, He invites us to come and walk out the storm with Him, reminding us that that very same "incomparably great power" that raised Him is available to all who believe (Ephesians 1:19). And when we, like Peter, lose sight of Him and become overwhelmed by the elements, He reaches out with love and compassion to lift us back up.

There is nothing you face today that is not already under His feet. And there is nothing you face that He won't empower you to get through either. *Where in your life do you need to be reminded that Jesus walks on water—and you can too?*

HE CALMED THE STORM TO A
WHISPER AND STILLED THE WAVES.
WHAT A BLESSING WAS THAT
STILLNESS AS HE BROUGHT THEM
SAFELY INTO HARBOUR!

PSALM 107:29–30 NLT

Father, I thank You for my water-walking Jesus. I
believe that You have placed all things under His
feet including my circumstances—nothing is too
hard for Him. I fix my eyes on Him, celebrating
the incomparably great power that is available
to me today.

God Doesn't Make Mistakes

EMILY

When we first moved to New Zealand, it took us a while to find a suitable alternative to replace our kids' beloved 'squash' drink. Essentially, we needed cordial, but New Zealand prices don't lend themselves to the frequent purchase of cordial!

We ended up settling on a powdered flavouring that you mix with water (once I could get past the whole powder situation). The advice on the packet said to dilute the powder with one litre of water. But when we did this, the potency and strength was just too much. We needed it to be less intense and added more water to make it weaker.

If you're anything like me, there may well have been times in your life where you've felt, or others have told you, that you are 'too much'. Too loud, too strong, too confident, too intense, too. . . different. Conversely, at times people might complain you are too nice, too shy, too quiet, too timid. It seems that whatever 'too' you are, there will be those who want to dilute you and make you less than you are.

But God doesn't make mistakes. And He didn't make any when He made you. You are fearfully and wonderfully made—personality included (Psalm 139). You are His workmanship (Ephesians 2:10), and He delights in you (Zechariah 3:17).

"Blessed is the one who trusts in the Lord, whose confidence is in Him" (Jeremiah 17:7). The next time you find others attempting to pour water over you to make you less than you are, remember that your confidence is in Christ, and you are blessed when you trust in Him. Despite others coming against you, you need not fear and can declare, like David, that you will be confident (Psalm 27:3). Why? Because "with Him on [your] side [you are] fearless, afraid of no one and nothing" (Psalm 27:1 MSG).

"Each person is given something to do that shows who God is: Everyone gets in on it, everyone benefits" (1 Corinthians 12:7 MSG). You have something to offer by being you, as you are, undiluted. Please don't let others miss out on what you have to bring. Keep being you!

FOR WE ARE GOD'S HANDIWORK, CREATED IN CHRIST JESUS TO DO GOOD WORKS, WHICH GOD PREPARED IN ADVANCE FOR US TO DO.

EPHESIANS 2:10

Father, I am blessed as I trust in You today. You delight in me, Your child, for I am fearfully and wonderfully made. I walk in confidence, knowing I am created with unique purpose and potential.

Offer Him Your 'Only'

AIMÉE

I had come away from a speaking engagement disappointed. Despite all my preparation and the expectation that I had felt leading up to it, on the night of the event I felt like I fell short. I wrestled with my weakness, feeling what I had offered up was not enough.

The next morning, a friend texted to see how the night had gone, and I confided in her the inadequacy of how I felt. Her wise response, "All we can do is offer up to Jesus our loaves and our fish for Him to use and to multiply."

It's a familiar story. The crowds stood before the disciples who had the seemingly impossible task of feeding them. The disciples wanted to send them away to find their own food, but Jesus insisted that they find them something to eat. In a remote location this was no easy task, and after doing what they could, they said to Jesus, "We have here only five loaves of bread and two fish." To which He responded, "Bring them here to me. . ." (Matthew 14:17-18).

Only.

How often is that our response to what God calls us to? How often do we feel inadequate for the tasks before us; that we aren't and don't have enough to meet the needs in front of us? To be the mum, the wife, the colleague, the. . . that we want to be? And Jesus simply says, "bring what you have to Me."

That day, a little boy's lunch fed a crowd that scholars believe may have exceeded twenty thousand once you added in the women and children. But here's the truly amazing thing: They weren't only fed, they were satisfied, *and* there were plenty of leftovers! A basket for each of the twelve disciples, in fact!

I am so grateful that God doesn't ask me to have enough on my own, but simply invites me to offer up my 'only', fully entrusting the outcome to Him. I can surrender all that I am and all that I do have to Him with the confidence that He will use it and make it fruitful; that it will not only satisfy the needs of those He calls me to minister to, but there will also be something leftover to minister to me.

What is Jesus asking you to bring to Him today?

I PLANTED THE SEED, APOLLOS WATERED IT, BUT GOD HAS BEEN MAKING IT GROW. SO NEITHER THE ONE WHO PLANTS NOR THE ONE WHO WATERS IS ANYTHING, BUT ONLY GOD, WHO MAKES THINGS GROW.

I CORINTHIANS 3:6-7

Father, I offer you my 'only' today. I believe that You are able to take it and use it and multiply it for Your glory. I trust You to bring the growth as I faithfully play my part.

Until the Day

EMILY

I like to get stuff done. Some say this is a positive thing, and others, well. . . just pray for my family! I've been reading a bit about patience and impatience recently, and the Merriam-Webster definition of the term 'impatient' is: 'not willing to wait for something or someone: not patient; wanting or eager to do something without waiting; showing that you do not want to wait: showing a lack of patience'.

Contrast this with two passages of Scripture: Joshua 6:10 and Luke 1:80. The first is when Joshua is giving the army the instructions for defeating Jericho. You probably know the story— they march around the city for six days, then on the seventh day go around it seven times and don't hold back on the noise. "But Joshua commanded the people, 'You shall not shout or make your voice heard, neither shall any word go out of your mouth, *until the day* I tell you to shout. Then you shall shout'" (Joshua 6:10 ESV).

The other verse is about John the Baptist growing up in the wilderness before entering his ministry: "And the child grew and became strong in spirit, and he was in the wilderness *until the day* of his public appearance to Israel" (Luke 1:80 ESV).

Do you notice the similarities? There were instructions, there was waiting, there was a seeming delay—*until the day.* Until the day when the walls fell down. Until the day when John was allowed to be with other people. Until the day the finances come through, you meet 'the one', or the prayer is answered. . .

It's no surprise that our culture of instant gratification and the immediacy of technology makes our society so impatient, but there's something about waiting 'until the day' that God can use for our growth and His glory.

There is a time for each and every purpose and plan that God has for us. It can be easy at times to think that God is not active or doesn't see or care about a particular desire or hope that we have. But we can trust that He is working out all things for good, even as we wait on this side of "until the day."

BUT DO NOT FORGET THIS ONE THING, DEAR FRIENDS: WITH THE LORD A DAY IS LIKE A THOUSAND YEARS, AND A THOUSAND YEARS ARE LIKE A DAY. THE LORD IS NOT SLOW IN KEEPING HIS PROMISE, AS SOME UNDERSTAND SLOWNESS.

2 PETER 3:8-9A

Father, I trust You that You are working all things for good. I wait patiently for You to bring to fruition Your promises for my life. Thank You that in the waiting You are preparing, growing, and equipping me that I might be in alignment with Your plans and purposes.

Whose Approval Are You After?

AIMÉE

We're meant to be getting out the door, but instead I'm frantically trying to fit my housework into five minutes: dishwasher loaded, benches clear, table wiped down, washing on, lounge tidy, a quick spot vacuum.

The kids are groaning at me—beeping the car horn even. The older one is texting me, "Hurry up Mum!"

I don't even really know who I'm cleaning up for. The person who 'might' pop in? *Am I hoping to give off the impression that I've got the art of housekeeping and parenting all figured out? That everything is under control?*

It's the same reason that everything gets thrown into the master bedroom when guests are coming and the door firmly shut on any 'mess'. (Don't tell me you've never done that!)

Lately, as I've found myself in this frame of mind, running around like a madwoman with my thoughts condemning me for all that is still undone, I've had Paul's words from Galatians 1 ringing in my ears: "Am I now trying to win the approval of men or of God? Or am I trying to please men? If I were still trying to please men, I would not be a servant of Christ" (v.10).

You see, it's not my cleaning that's the problem but the driving force behind it. The search for approval and praise still often has me looking in the wrong places. It causes me to strive to earn what Christ has already given me and now invites me to stand firm in: grace, freedom, love, acceptance, belonging, and purpose.

But when I get caught up in trying to prove myself to those around me; in bending my priorities to reflect theirs, I miss His. I miss the things He is inviting me to partner with Him in. I miss the moments He is inviting me to enjoy. I miss the rest and peace that He invites me to live out of.

I can't promise you I will never hide my mess again, but this recovering perfectionist is daily seeking to find her approval and her priorities in His presence. *Where is God inviting you to cease striving and instead serve Him?*

I HAVE BEEN CRUCIFIED WITH CHRIST AND I NO LONGER LIVE, BUT CHRIST LIVES IN ME. THE LIFE I NOW LIVE IN THE BODY, I LIVE BY FAITH IN THE SON OF GOD, WHO LOVED ME AND GAVE HIMSELF FOR ME.

GALATIANS 2:20

Father, I lay aside my striving today to receive all that Christ has done for me. I will not exhaust myself seeking the fickle approval of men; I am Your servant. You are the One that I live for.

Forerunner

EMILY

Have you ever noticed how raindrops move on the other side of a window? Assume for a moment that the goal of the raindrop is to travel to the bottom of the window. Some drops manage to move a little but then get stuck. They never quite reach their destination.

However, when one raindrop finds another one, they join together, and their combined power and momentum allows them to move further and faster. As soon as some raindrops are moving, it's easier for others to join the momentum because a pathway, a channel, has been carved through the grime on the window pane.

It's as though these raindrops instinctively know they need to seek each other out if they're to reach their destination. The drops aren't supposed to go it alone. *How do they find each other?* It's easier to follow a path when someone has already travelled ahead of you.

I was running an unknown trail recently. It was hard to work out exactly which way to go at times because the path was so overgrown. Yet, every so often a bright pink ribbon was tied around a tree, illuminating the path ahead of me. Someone who knew the way had gone before me and marked out the trail. I had confidence in my next steps because I trusted the one who had carved out the path ahead.

Jesus has gone before us. He is our forerunner (Hebrews 6:20) and rear guard (Isaiah 52:12), and He has left us a trail to follow. When we don't know the way; when we're not sure which way to turn next; when we are overwhelmed by life, we can trust the pink ribbons Jesus has left for us. As we read in Deuteronomy 31:8, "The Lord himself goes before you and will be with you; he will never leave you nor forsake you. Do not be afraid; do not be discouraged."

We aren't supposed to go it alone either. We're all members of His body, part of the Church. When many raindrops gather together they have much more power and impact potential, and they're more likely to reach their intended destination! The same goes for us too.

WE HAVE THIS HOPE AS AN ANCHOR FOR THE SOUL, FIRM AND SECURE. IT ENTERS THE INNER SANCTUARY BEHIND THE CURTAIN, WHERE OUR FORERUNNER, JESUS, HAS ENTERED ON OUR BEHALF. HE HAS BECOME A HIGH PRIEST FOREVER, IN THE ORDER OF MELCHIZEDEK.

HEBREWS 6:19-20

Father, I thank You that You have gone before me. I fix my eyes on Jesus, following the path He has marked out for me, and playing my part in the Church so that, united, we reach our destination together. I will not be afraid or discouraged for I know You are always with me.

A Different Understanding

AIMÉE

Some days feel like they were taken straight from the pages of "Alexander and the Terrible, Horrible, No Good, Very Bad Day"—and we'd like nothing more than to join Alexander in running away to Timbuktu.

Alexander's terrible day is one of my son's favourite stories to read at bedtime, but lately he's been making me read it differently—I have to make it 'happy'. The events have to unfold more or less in the same way, but Alexander must have a different understanding of them. He must see the day as being "fantastic, wonderful, and very good—the best day ever." And running off to Timbuktu is most definitely not an option. This exercise in filtering Alexander's day through a different lens has had me evaluating how I perceive my own life and whether I need to allow God to correct my vision.

In the book of Habakkuk, we read a dialogue between Habakkuk and God. Habakkuk is complaining to God, asking Him *all* the questions, and the Lord is graciously answering him. After voicing a stream of concerns, Habakkuk pauses to say this:

> "I will stand my watch
> And set myself on the rampart,
> And watch to see what He will say to me,
> And what I will answer when I am corrected."
> (Habakkuk 2:1, NKJV)

Habakkuk was in a season that, quite honestly, I would have been complaining about too. It made Alexander's day look like a walk in the park. Yet he made room for God to correct his understanding, acknowledging that perhaps his understanding of what was unfolding around him wasn't quite accurate. And as he pauses to allow himself to see God's perspective, the revelation that unfolds leads him from a place of despair to steadfast hope. His questions give way to a declaration that he will be joyful in God his Saviour; in the One who gives him the strength to endure (Habakkuk 3:18-19).

Where in your life do you need to allow God to reframe your understanding? Allow your heart to echo the prayer of Habakkuk, and let God lead you back to hope.

THOUGH THE FIG TREE DOES NOT
BUD AND THERE ARE NO GRAPES
ON THE VINES, THOUGH THE OLIVE
CROP FAILS AND THE FIELDS
PRODUCE NO FOOD, THOUGH
THERE ARE NO SHEEP IN THE PEN
AND NO CATTLE IN THE STALLS, YET
I WILL REJOICE IN THE LORD, I WILL
BE JOYFUL IN GOD MY SAVIOUR.

HABAKKUK 3:17–18

Father, I come into Your presence to
watch and to listen. I am willing for you to
reshape my understanding. You are
my Sovereign Lord and I trust You.

Just Do It

EMILY

Do you ever lie in bed in the morning wishing you didn't have to get up, because you've got a list as long as your arm of things you need to get done? Maybe it's as mundane as cleaning the bathroom or perhaps it's a more meaningful task that will impact others (not that cleaning the bathroom doesn't impact others!). Either way, something—be it apathy or dread— holds you back from throwing off the covers and facing the tasks of the day.

If I said, "Just Do It" to you, you'd know immediately which brand that represents. *Why is it that this decades-old Nike slogan has had so much success?* The truth is, it speaks to everyone. From the richest to the poorest, from the most athletically tuned individual to the couch potato; it calls us to rise up and believe that if they can do it, then *yes, I can do it too.*

But sometimes 'doing it' requires help. It requires another to come alongside. It requires encouragement, expertise, or simply knowing that you're not facing the task alone. Sometimes you just can't do it by yourself. In the book of Ezra, Shekaniah knew that the Israelites needed both encouragement and strength in numbers if they were going to follow through on the task of repenting and doing what was right, and avoid potential judgement from the Lord. While Ezra wept, prayed, and confessed on behalf of the people, Shekaniah addressed him,

> "Arise, for it is your task, and we are with you; be strong and do it"
> (Ezra 10:4 ESV).

The beauty of this exhortation is that we also have the truth of the New Testament to hold onto. Whatever task you are facing, Jesus has promised that He is with us to the very end of the age—and that includes cleaning bathrooms! He has equipped us with every good thing needed for the purposes He has called us to (Hebrews 13:21), and promises to complete the work in us that He has started (Philippians 1:6). And when we are weak, we get to be strong *in* Him.

What is God calling you to today? Rise up, know that He is with you, go forth in His strength, and just do it!

"RISE UP; THIS MATTER IS IN YOUR HANDS. WE WILL SUPPORT YOU, SO TAKE COURAGE AND DO IT."

EZRA 10:4

Father, willingly, I will rise and attend to the tasks You have placed in front of me knowing that You are with me. Equipped with everything good that I could need, I know You will complete the work You have begun in me.

Choose Your Own Adventure

AIMÉE

Every day is filled with a myriad of decisions. Some we make almost automatically, but others weigh heavy. We want to get it right. We're afraid that if we get it wrong, perhaps we'll miss out on what God has for us.

For me, these fears coupled with my deep-seated desire to honour God became somewhat paralysing. Then, facing an impossible decision, I heard God whisper, *It's okay Aimee, if you think you can keep going that's great; if you need to stop, that's okay too, either way I love you.* It was then that I came to understand there isn't always 'one' right decision; oftentimes there are several good options and God trusts us to choose.

God is sovereign and all-powerful, yet He has also chosen to partner with us. We are not powerless in this partnership and it does not reduce our lives to a predetermined script. Made in the image of God, we have been given the ability to think and feel and dream and create. God wants us to use these abilities which is why He not only trusts us to choose, He also empowers us to choose well.

It's a bit like those 'Choose your own Adventure' books where every few pages you're presented with different options, and where you decide to go next determines the story's end. In some editions there are up to forty possible endings! Rather than having one fixed ending, I've discovered there are a variety of paths we could go down and they *all* have the potential to have God-honouring conclusions However, the paradox of this freedom is that it requires complete surrender. It requires us to be what Paul describes as a "living sacrifice" (Romans 12:1).

Such a surrender is a safe-guard to the incredible freedom we have in Christ. God can always work with a heart that genuinely desires to serve and honour Him—even if we misstep or misinterpret what His Word says, He is big enough to redirect us and get us back on track. As we surrender our lives to Him, our hearts and minds are transformed and renewed so that when life feels like a multi-choice test, we are able to recognise the paths that hold what is "good, pleasing, and perfect" (Romans 12:2). Only then, can we confidently exercise our freedom to choose.

What adventures are waiting for you to choose them?

DO NOT CONFORM TO THE PATTERN OF THIS WORLD, BUT BE TRANSFORMED BY THE RENEWING OF YOUR MIND. THEN YOU WILL BE ABLE TO TEST AND APPROVE WHAT GOD'S WILL IS—HIS GOOD, PLEASING AND PERFECT WILL.

ROMANS 12:2

Father, I am ready to go on an adventure with You today! My mind is daily being renewed as I present myself to You as a living sacrifice. You empower me to discern Your good, pleasing, and perfect will, and the paths I choose honour You.

Let Him Lead

EMILY

"STOP BEING IN CHARGE OF ME!" I heard one child scream at the other. I sighed. Their words triggered flashbacks of similar words expressed with equal levels of frustration from my own childhood. No one likes to be controlled. No one wants to have someone else tell them what to do, dominate them, or dictate to them—and we don't even need siblings for this revelation.

Yet I wonder, *Do we ever subconsciously say this to God?* Holding tightly onto any semblance of control and fighting Him for any opportunity to take the reins, there are times I find myself silently screaming, "Stop being in charge of me!" when things don't seem to pan out the way I want them to.

We were born for freedom, yet we often try to use that freedom to serve ourselves, to go our own way, to foster and nurture pride, arrogance, selfishness, unforgiveness, or any number of sins. But "those things result in death!... Now that [we] have been set free from sin and have become slaves of God, the benefit [we] reap leads to holiness" (Romans 6:21b-22).

Our natural human self will always revolt against the idea of being controlled. Yet, if we want to know life in all its fullness, the topsy-turvy Kingdom way says we must give up our lives in pursuit of serving Jesus. I'm all with my child who rebelled against their sibling trying to be the parent and 'play God', but we actually have a God who needs us to let go of our control if we're going to have anything close to the life we desire. Jesus explained this to His disciples:

"Anyone who intends to come with me has to let me lead. You're not in the driver's seat; I am. Don't run from suffering; embrace it. Follow me and I'll show you how. Self-help is no help at all. Self-sacrifice is the way, my way, to finding yourself, your true self" (Matthew 16:24-26 MSG).

If we want to journey with Jesus, we need to stop holding onto our substandard idea of freedom and instead surrender to His leading. Take a moment with Holy Spirit to check that you're not holding onto any areas of your life or heart, and instead embrace the Jesus way, the servant way, the "I'm-not-in-charge" way.

FOR WHOEVER WANTS TO SAVE
THEIR LIFE WILL LOSE IT, BUT
WHOEVER LOSES THEIR LIFE FOR
ME WILL FIND IT.

MATTHEW 16:25

Father, I relinquish my desire for control and submit to Your leading. I surrender my faulty thinking about what it means to be free and embrace Jesus' gift of true freedom. I will not pursue the things that lead to death but spend my life in service for Him.

Change Your Mind

AIMÉE

"But she..."

This is a common response in our household when I correct one of my children—rather than accepting responsibility, they're quick to blame someone else for their failure.

I understand this tendency. I don't think anyone particularly enjoys admitting they were wrong. Having to confront our failures and inadequacies can be difficult, and ignoring them or sweeping them under the carpet can feel easier—at least initially. I've learned the hard way that what we try to cover up festers, but what we allow God to cover over is transformed.

In Acts 3, Peter exhorted those who had just witnessed him and John heal a crippled man to, "repent and return, so that your sins may be wiped away, in order that times of refreshing may come from the presence of the Lord" (v.19 NASB).

Repentance is not the most popular of words or concepts, yet without it we are robbed of God's refreshing presence. Sin cannot go unchecked, otherwise the dirt and mess of our lives obstruct the flow of His Living Water, and we find ourselves dry and empty. Yes, repentance and refreshing do indeed go hand-in-hand.

Repentance itself simply means 'to change one's mind [for the better]; heartily to amend with the abhorrence of one's past sin'. In order to change our minds, we have to first acknowledge that something is broken and that there is a better way—God's way. Our salvation begins with repentance, and our sanctification—the process of becoming like Christ—requires us to keep allowing God to change our thinking. Repentance is not an isolated event but a lifestyle that we are called to embrace.

There is a lightness that enters our hearts when we keep short accounts with God; a freedom that comes when we allow Him to correct us and bear the heavy burden of our sin. As you enter a new day, allow God to cleanse you of the grime that has accumulated. Tarry in His presence and allow Him to examine your heart and show you a better way—a refreshing way.

GOD, I INVITE YOUR SEARCHING GAZE INTO MY HEART. EXAMINE ME THROUGH AND THROUGH. . . SEE IF THERE IS ANY PATH OF PAIN I'M WALKING ON, AND LEAD ME BACK TO YOUR GLORIOUS, EVERLASTING WAY – THE PATH THAT BRINGS ME BACK TO YOU.

PSALM 139:23-24 TPT

Father, I pause and acknowledge that there is a better way, Your way. I confess that I have fallen short of Your standards and I embrace Christ's extravagant gift of forgiveness and grace. I align my life and ways with Yours; I want to walk on the paths that keep me close to You.

Don't Fade Away

EMILY

I often write notes in the margins of my Bible: revelations when reading passages, fresh insights, links to other verses, illustrations for future talks, things I think God is saying. . . Well, consider my dismay when I opened my Bible to discover that 380 pages of notes had disappeared! The ink had literally vanished from the page.

I was so disappointed in the ephemeral nature of the ink. I had been using such a pretty pink pen. But what the pen possessed in prettiness, it lacked in permanence. *Why didn't it stand the test of time? Why was it that, when left next to the heater, the rising temperature made my notes fade away?*

Luckily, I was able to hold each page—yes all 380 of them—up to the light and just about make out the indentations that the nib had left on the page, so I could go back over my notes with a more permanent pen. It was a powerful lesson in the importance of permanence—one that can be applied to our faith too.

The apostle Peter tells us that, "These [all kinds of trials] have come so that the proven genuineness of your faith—of greater worth than gold, which perishes even though refined by fire—may result in praise, glory and honour when Jesus Christ is revealed" (1 Peter 1:7).

It's true that when the temperature of life rises, our faith is tested. When trials come and heat up our lives, it puts our faith to the test: *Will it fade away or endure and remain strong to the end?*

Our faith isn't about what it looks like on the outside—it's not about how pretty our lives appear to be. We shouldn't be living lives of pink ink! If we want our lives to result in praise, glory, and honour then we're going to need to embrace the trials that refine and purify our faith rather than shrink back and disappear when the temperature heats up.

Next time you feel the temperature increasing, don't despair. Instead, celebrate that this is a moment for your faith to display its lasting power and permanence, bringing praise to the very One who gave you that gift of faith in the first place.

PURE GOLD PUT IN THE FIRE
COMES OUT OF IT PROVED PURE:
GENUINE FAITH PUT THROUGH THIS
SUFFERING COMES OUT PROVED
GENUINE. WHEN JESUS WRAPS
THIS ALL UP, IT'S YOUR FAITH, NOT
YOUR GOLD, THAT GOD WILL HAVE
ON DISPLAY AS EVIDENCE OF HIS
VICTORY.

I PETER 1:7 MSG

Father, I don't want a faith that fades away under pressure. I embrace the testing seasons and stay the course knowing You are refining and purifying my faith. Even when I walk through fire, I bring You glory and honour as I hold fast to You.

Relish the Season

AIMÉE

When I was first given the opportunity to preach, I tried to cram into each message every. single. thing. that God was teaching me at the time. There was an underlying fear that if I didn't say it now, I might not get to say it at all.

Often we live our lives the same way. Driven by the fear that if we don't 'have' it now, we'll never have it at all, we try and fit everything in at once, continually adding to our already too-full schedules to avoid the feeling that we're missing out or what we're doing is unimportant. However, from my experience, trying to 'have it all' simultaneously only results in exhaustion and a general sense of dissatisfaction; it leaves us perpetually looking to the future and can cause us to devalue the people and purposes God has entrusted us with *now*.

Solomon offers us this wisdom in Ecclesiastes 3: "There is a time for everything, and a season for every activity under the heavens" (v.1). Some 'activities' are instinctively more appealing to us than others. We prefer laughing over weeping, gathering over scattering, and building over tearing down. But Solomon reminds us that God "has made everything beautiful in its time" (v.11). There is a beauty that marks out our days when we identify the purpose of a season and are present to it.

As Solomon continues to ponder the seasons that shape our lives, he concludes, "I know that there is nothing better for people than to be happy and to do good while they live. That each of them may eat and drink, and find satisfaction in all their toil—this is the gift of God" (vv.12-13).

I find such freedom in Solomon's reflections. They encourage me that there will be a time and a season to give expression to the things I carry in my heart, even if it isn't now. This enables me to enjoy where God has me while also allowing me to keep my dreams alive. But his words also remind me that satisfaction doesn't have to be deferred. When I realise I don't have to do it all at once, there is a slowing of pace within my heart that enables me to "enjoy the fruits of [my] labour"(v.13 NLT)—just as God intended.

What season are you in? Relish it. Be present to it. Honour its purpose in your life, and find rest in the truth that there is a time for *everything*.

TRUST IN THE LORD AND DO GOOD;
DWELL IN THE LAND AND ENJOY
SAFE PASTURE. TAKE DELIGHT IN
THE LORD, AND HE WILL GIVE YOU
THE DESIRES OF YOUR HEART.

PSALM 37:3-4

Father, I resist the pressure to have it all and do
it all. I slow the pace of my heart to keep in step
with You, knowing that I cannot miss out when
I am present and obedient to Your purposes.
I relish the season You have me in knowing
You make all things beautiful in their time.

Do Not Be Deceived

EMILY

I've spent many a weekend learning about stunts and fighting in film and television. It's a fascinating and physically full-on experience. I also discovered that one of the key things that makes for a good stunt or fight on TV is deception.

Typically deception is a bad thing. However in the world of stunts, it is necessary for the audience to be deceived to ensure the stunt performers are not hurt and the fight looks real on camera. We need clever camera angles, technological tricks, and highly skilled performers to fool us into thinking something is happening when it's not. Otherwise people would be seriously injured.

When Paul is writing to the Galatians he warns them of the dangers of deceiving themselves. Deception for the stunt performer is all about looking after their fellow cast members and team. Deception for the Galatians, however, was all about believing they were carrying each other's burdens and looking out for one another when actually they weren't at all.

"Do not be deceived," Paul warns in (Galatians 6:7 ESV), you will reap what you sow. If you are performing a stunt or a fight and you think only about yourself, then you and others will end up struggling, wounded, and possibly even dead. It's a team mission. If you live your Christian life thinking only of yourself then the same outcomes may apply!

Paul exhorts believers to "take advantage of every opportunity to be a blessing to others" (Galatians 6:10 TPT). We should not deceive ourselves into thinking that we're living life for others when really we only have our best interests at heart. Instead, we should, "Bear one another's burdens, and so fulfil the law of Christ" (Galatians 6:2 ESV).

As a stunt performer, no one is exempt from the responsibility of looking after the team, considering the impact of their actions on those around them, and ensuring the setting is safe and everyone is accounted for and equipped for the task ahead.

The same goes for us as Christ followers. Don't deceive yourself. This is a team mission.

DO NOT BE FOOLED: YOU CANNOT CHEAT GOD. A PERSON HARVESTS ONLY WHAT HE PLANTS. IF HE PLANTS TO SATISFY HIS SINFUL SELF, HIS SINFUL SELF WILL BRING HIM ETERNAL DEATH. BUT IF HE PLANTS TO PLEASE THE SPIRIT, HE WILL RECEIVE ETERNAL LIFE FROM THE SPIRIT.

GALATIANS 6:7–8 ICB

Father, I check my heart today. I will not just look out for my own interests but recognise that I am part of a team—Your team. I will bear others' burdens and take every opportunity to be a blessing.

Our Advantage

AIMÉE

Before the invention of the smartphone, my brother bought me an iPod Shuffle. He thought I'd enjoy listening to my worship music and sermons on it. Confession: I've never used it. I've owned this incredibly capable little device for well over a decade and I've not once reaped the benefits of it. *Why?* I didn't (and still don't) understand how it works.

Our experience with Holy Spirit can be somewhat similar. We're usually able to wrap our heads around the Father and Son, but Holy Spirit can often feel like an enigma. Because of this, we risk missing out on experiencing the benefit of this incredible gift we have been given.

Knowing how critical it was that we understand just who Holy Spirit is and what His role is in our lives, Jesus spent much of His last hours with the disciples teaching them about the One that He said was *for our best* and *to our advantage* (John 16:7, NLT & NKJV). Holy Spirit, He tells us, is our *paraklētos*—our Counsellor, Advocate, and Comforter (John 14:16).

When the enemy accuses and attacks, Holy Spirit is our Advocate. When we need someone to stand in the gap for us or we don't know how to pray, Holy Spirit is our intercessor, praying through us and for us (Romans 8:26). When we're in distress, He is our Comforter and succourer. When we don't know what to do next, He is our Counsellor and teacher, the One who leads us into all truth (John 16:12).

Holy Spirit has been sent to continue the truth of Emmanuel, *God with us*. Yet unlike Jesus, who in taking on our form was constrained to one place at one time, Holy Spirit is able to be with *all of us* at all times because He is *within us*. This gift of the indwelling presence of God Himself means that we are never alone. We receive this gift, simply by believing that Jesus is who He said He was: "*the* way, *the* truth, and *the* life" (John 14:6). But we experience the full benefit of it through obedience—through yielding and surrendering our lives to the One in whom we believe. As we do, Holy Spirit is able to move unhindered in us and through us.

Don't let fear of the unknown cause you to miss out on your advantage. Allow Holy Spirit full access to your life and watch as He comes alongside you to empower the life God has called you to.

NEVERTHELESS, I TELL YOU THE TRUTH: IT IS TO YOUR ADVANTAGE THAT I GO AWAY, FOR IF I DO NOT GO AWAY, THE HELPER WILL NOT COME TO YOU. BUT IF I GO, I WILL SEND HIM TO YOU.

JOHN 16:7 ESV

Father, I believe that Jesus is the way, the truth, and the life. I yield my life to Him and receive the gift and help of Holy Spirit. He is my advantage and I stand in awe at the wonder that Your very Spirit is within me empowering me today.

How Much More?

EMILY

A Canadian airline company once ran a memorable festive marketing campaign. As they boarded, passengers were asked what they most wanted for Christmas. When the flight touched down, gifts ranging from train sets and dolls to new snowboards and 50" TVs were given to the passengers on arrival at their destination. Those who asked for socks looked a little despondent—if only they'd asked for more! The promotional video concluded, "the guests never expected what they asked for from Saint Nick to actually appear."

Spiritually, I often feel like the most I ever ask God for is socks. The bare minimum—only what I need and what is necessary. I don't get my hopes up asking for more because, if I'm truly honest, I don't expect it to appear.

When did we stop trusting in the goodness of God?

In John 4:10, Jesus tells the woman at the well, "If you only knew the gift God has for you and who you are speaking to, you would ask" (NLT). If we only knew the expanse of the storehouse from which God can give, we might start asking for more than socks.

My children are masters of asking. They do not hold back. If they want something, they'll ask for it. They know they might not always get it—but they'll ask anyway because sometimes Mum might surprise them and let them eat chocolate for breakfast. If we know how to give good things to our children, "how much more will [our] Father who is in heaven give good things to those who ask him!" (Matthew 7:11b ESV).

How much more? We need to get better at asking. Unlike making asks of our earthly parents, when we ask Jesus, we are asking the One "who is able to do far more abundantly than all that we ask or think" (Ephesians 3:20 ESV).

So let's ask big for our communities, for the schools our kids attend, and for the colleagues we share a cubicle with. Let's ask big for our homes and families, for the politicians and leaders of our countries. Let's ask big for the sick, the destitute, and the lowly.

Don't settle for socks. Ask big!

JESUS REPLIED, "IF YOU ONLY KNEW
THE GIFT GOD HAS FOR YOU AND
WHO YOU ARE SPEAKING TO, YOU
WOULD ASK ME, AND I WOULD
GIVE YOU LIVING WATER."

JOHN 4:10 NLT

Father, I believe You are the God of abundance
who longs to pour blessing into my life. Today, I
trust that You desire to move in and through me.
I thank You, and I give You all my praise. I will not
hold back in asking for Your Kingdom, power,
and glory to come on earth as it is in Heaven.

About the Authors

Emily

Emily is a certified coach, speaker, author, and pastor with a particular passion for seeing God's people 'grow and go'. Driven by the conviction that God's Word brings life and freedom, Em preaches and writes for transformation and growth within the Christian context. She is committed to helping believers get 'unstuck' and discover everything God has for them. Married to a phenomenal specimen of man (Dan) with three spectacular works of God's creativity (her kids), you can connect with Emily for coaching, speaking, or just to say "hi" at emtyler.com

Her mug of choice is any mug from the iamsomanythings.com range (she's an avid collector of them all)! Bright, bold, and colourful, these fine bone china mugs are printed with biblically-based identity declarations making them weighty in truth and size.

Aimée

A pastor and writer, Aimée is a lover of God's Word. Passionate about helping people understand the truth of the Scriptures so they can live in the fullness of all God has planned and purposed for their lives, she's a speaker and the author of But I Flourish, and has also written nine Bible studies (and counting). These days you're most likely to find her writing in the margins, with a cup of strong black coffee in hand as she and her hubby Dave juggle the beautiful chaos of family life and try to keep up with their four kids–and each other! Connect with Aimée on Instagram at @aimeerwalker.

Her mug of choice is a custom made tumbler from a local New Zealand potter engraved with the word 'flourish' in honour of her first book. Filled with coffee that never quite gets finished, it's a daily reminder to her that in Christ she can grow and thrive in any season.

About The Devoted Collective

Our vision is simple: to serve God with wholehearted devotion, fulfilling the command Christ gave us to love the Lord with all our heart, soul, and mind (Matthew 22:37).

We want to love God with all that we are, right where we are. In order to do that, The Devoted Collective is anchored in three core disciplines modelled for us in Acts 2:42: devotion to the Word, to community, and to prayer. It is our heart's desire that, through committing to these practices with us, you will experience the richness of all God intends for your life as you come to know Him more intimately.

The more we know God, the more we can't help but love Him; and the more we love Him, the more we desire to serve Him—and that's what wholehearted devotion is all about.

Connect with us on social media @thedevotedcollective
www.thedevotedcollective.org

Join Us in the Devoted Community

We want to invite you into a place to know and be known, a place to belong, a place where you are part of something both unimaginably expansive and wondrously intimate: the family of God.

We want to invite you to be part of The Devoted Community.

The Devoted Community is about belonging—belonging more fully to God and to one another. It's about a dedicated place away from the busyness and noise of social media. It's about a place where you are seen and known; a place to gain wisdom and knowledge; a place to explore and embrace; a place to go higher and deeper and wider in God in the company of new friends and chosen family.

Within our community you will find:

Bible reading plans
Prayer threads and small groups
Dedicated mentors and monthly lives with Aimee and Emily
Exclusive content and topical modules
Believers seeking the heart of God—just like you

Who is it for?

If you are hungry and thirsty for more of Jesus. . .
If you desire to go deeper in your faith. . .
If you want to take hold of all the promises of God. . .
If you long to enjoy Him all the days of your life. . .
If you are looking for others who feel the same. . .

. . .then The Devoted Community is for you.

Come and belong: www.thedevotedcollective.org/community

9 780473 659226